Franklin
a peur de l'orage

Paulette Bourgeois • Brenda Clark

Pour ma voisine, Amanda - *P. B.*

Pour ma mère, qui a encore peur de l'orage - *B.C.*

Franklin est une marque de Kids Can Press Ltd.
Publié pour la première fois en 1998 par Kids Can Press Ltd.,
Toronto, Ontario, Canada, sous le titre de *Franklin and the Thunderstorm.*

Les illustrations ont été réalisées avec l'aide de Shelley Southern
et Muriel Hughes Wood

ISBN 978.2.01.393255.4
Dépôt légal : Juillet 2011 - Édition 01
Imprimé en France par Jean-Lamour
Loi n° 49-956 du 16 juillet 1949
sur les publications destinées à la jeunesse.

Franklin
a peur de l'orage

Paulette Bourgeois • Brenda Clark

Adaptation française de Cécile Beaucourt

DEUX COQS D'OR

Franklin sait compter jusqu'à cent et nouer ses lacets comme un grand. Il peut réciter par cœur tous les mois de l'année, et même les saisons. Il sait lire la température sur le thermomètre et il jette chaque jour un coup d'œil au baromètre.

Il faut dire que si Franklin s'intéresse autant à la météo, c'est parce qu'il a peur de l'orage.

Aujourd'hui, il a prévu de retrouver ses amis chez Raffin le renardeau. Mais dehors, le ciel est de plus en plus noir et les nuages de plus en plus bas.

« Peut-être que je ferais mieux de ne pas y aller, dit Franklin à sa maman.

– La pluie ne va pas tomber tout de suite. À mon avis, tu as largement le temps d'arriver chez Raffin avant l'averse », répond-elle.

Franklin se met en route. Mais même avec ses bottes et son parapluie, il n'est pas très rassuré.

Il marche aussi vite qu'il peut, sans quitter le ciel des yeux. Les nuages filent à toute allure et le vent souffle méchamment.

Franklin ne se sent pas très bien.

Quand il arrive enfin chez Raffin, il trouve son ami qui joue dehors.

« Tu ne crois pas qu'on devrait rentrer ? » lui demande Franklin en montrant le ciel avec inquiétude.

Mais Raffin, lui, n'a pas peur. L'air effrayé de Franklin le fait plutôt rire.

« Pas tout de suite, dit-il. J'adore regarder les nuages et sentir le vent souffler. C'est rigolo !

– Moi, ça me fait peur », avoue Franklin.

Lili le castor, Arnaud l'escargot et Hubert le faucon les rejoignent pour jouer.

« Regardez, je suis tout ébouriffé ! s'écrie Raffin.

– Et moi, mes plumes sont toutes gonflées ! dit Hubert en riant.

– Hum hum… je crois que ça sent l'orage… » dit Lili en souriant, le nez au vent.

Franklin ne voit vraiment pas ce qu'il y a de drôle.

Le vent est de plus en plus violent.

« Wouaou ! » crie Hubert qui s'envole et se met à faire des loopings dans les courants d'air.

Franklin retient son chapeau en tremblant. Il fait très sombre. Les premières grosses gouttes s'écrasent sur le sol.

« Cette fois, on ferait vraiment mieux de rentrer, dit Franklin.

– Oh non, dit Raffin, suivez-moi ! »

Vite, vite, ils se réfugient dans la cabane pour être au sec.

La maman de Raffin les appelle :

« Il faut rentrer !

– Ne t'inquiète pas, lui crie Raffin, on est dans l'arbre. »

Mais sa maman les rejoint aussitôt.

« Il ne faut jamais rester près d'un arbre pendant un orage, dit-elle. La foudre tombe d'abord sur ce qui est haut. Vous risquez d'être blessés. »

De l'arbre jusqu'à la maison, Franklin court sans lâcher la main de la maman de Raffin.

Ils sont juste rentrés lorsqu'une grande lumière traverse le ciel en zigzaguant.

« Un éclair ! » crie Franklin.

Il est mort de peur.

BAAOOUUUM !

Il hurle : « Le tonnerre ! »

« Ne t'inquiète pas, Franklin, lui disent ses amis. On est en sécurité, ici. »

Mais Franklin s'est caché tout au fond de sa carapace.

Il ne veut pas sortir quand la maman de Raffin apporte le goûter.

Et il ne veut toujours pas montrer le bout de son nez quand ses amis lui proposent de jouer.

Soudain, après un énorme coup de tonnerre, la lumière s'éteint.

« Ne craignez rien, dit la maman de Raffin en allumant une lampe-torche et des bougies. Tu ne veux vraiment pas sortir de ta carapace ? demande-t-elle à Franklin.

– Non, merci », marmonne-t-il.

« N’aie pas peur, dit Hubert. Tout ce bruit, ce ne sont que les géants des nuages qui jouent de la batterie.

– C’est vrai ? demande Franklin en pointant le bout de son nez.

– Bien sûr que non, rigole Arnaud, ce bruit-là, c’est quand les géants jouent au bowling. »

« Et les éclairs, alors ? demande Franklin en sortant de sa carapace.

– Bah, dit Hubert, ce sont les géants des nuages qui n'arrêtent pas d'allumer et d'éteindre la lumière.

– À mon avis, c'est plutôt qu'ils sont en train de se balancer aux lustres », rétorque Raffin.

Franklin éclate de rire.

« Des géants ! N'importe quoi ! s'écrie Lili. M. Hibou a dit qu'un éclair est une grosse décharge électrique qui va du ciel vers la terre. La décharge est tellement forte que l'air qui l'entoure fait BOUM ! et c'est ça le tonnerre.

– C'est bizarre ! » dit Franklin.

Il n'a plus peur maintenant. Il joue même à faire des ombres chinoises avec la lampe-torche. Petit à petit, les éclairs s'espacent. Le tonnerre n'est plus qu'un faible grondement dans le lointain et la pluie s'arrête de tomber. La lumière revient.

« L'orage est fini ! dit Raffin. Allez, on va jouer dehors.

– Regarde, s'écrie Franklin, un arc-en-ciel ! »

« Moi, je sais pourquoi l'orage est fini, dit Franklin. Les géants savent qu'il y a toujours un trésor au pied d'un arc-en-ciel, et ils sont partis à sa recherche. »

Son explication fait sourire tous ses amis… même Lili.

Gillian Wearing and Claude Cahun

Behind the mask,
another mask

Gillian Wearing and Claude Cahun

Behind the mask,
another mask

Sarah Howgate

With an essay by Dawn Ades
and an interview with Gillian Wearing

National Portrait Gallery, London

Published in Great Britain by
National Portrait Gallery Publications
St Martin's Place, London WC2H 0HE

Published to accompany the exhibition *Gillian Wearing and Claude Cahun: Behind the mask, another mask* at the National Portrait Gallery, London, from 9 March to 29 May 2017.

Exhibition organised in collaboration with Gillian Wearing.

This exhibition has been made possible by the provision of insurance through the Government Indemnity Scheme. The National Portrait Gallery, London, would like to thank HM Government for providing Government Indemnity, and the Department for Culture, Media and Sport and Arts Council England for arranging the indemnity.

Every purchase supports the National Portrait Gallery, London. For a complete catalogue of current publications, please write to the National Portrait Gallery at the address above, or visit our website at www.npg.org.uk/publications

ISBN 978 1 85514 750 8

A catalogue record for this book is available from the British Library.

10 9 8 7 6 5 4 3 2 1

Managing Editor: Christopher Tinker
Editor: Andrew Roff
Copy-editor: Helen Armitage
Picture research: Mark Lynch
Production Manager: Ruth Müller-Wirth
Design: Praline (Sarah Krebietke, David Tanguy)

Printed and bound in Italy

Front jacket: *Me as Cahun holding a mask of my face* by Gillian Wearing, 2012 (detail of cat.6)
Back jacket: *Self-portrait (as Elle in* Barbe-Bleue*)* by Claude Cahun, 1929 (cat.65)
Front cover: *Self-portrait* from 'I am in training don't kiss me' series by Claude Cahun, c.1927 (detail of cat.5)
Previous page: Cat.1 *Me: Me* by Gillian Wearing, 1991/2016

The National Portrait Gallery's Spring Season is sponsored by Herbert Smith Freehills

COCKAYNE
The London Community Foundation

Notes All uncited quotations by Gillian Wearing are taken from conversations between Wearing and Sarah Howgate conducted in London on 28 January and 11 February 2016, which appear in edited form on pages 160–73.

In the catalogue section, names are abbreviated as follows: Gillian Wearing as GW; Claude Cahun as CC; and Marcel Moore as MM.

Contents

Director's foreword

In 1930, Claude Cahun wrote of her inimitable work: 'Under this mask, another mask. I will never finish removing all these faces'– an observation we have adapted to give this exhibition its evocative title. Gillian Wearing and Claude Cahun are pioneering artists, whose work, although separated by several decades, addresses similarly compelling themes of gender, identity and masquerade, articulated through photography and performance. Photographs taken by Cahun in private, often in collaboration with her partner and stepsister, Marcel Moore, are compared and contrasted with those of Wearing, some made in direct response to Cahun's, to create a resonant and thought-provoking intergenerational dialogue between the two artists.

At a time when issues relating to gender and identity are particularly pertinent, this exhibition of Cahun's and Wearing's extraordinary images is especially relevant. Living in German-occupied Jersey, Cahun endured great hardship but continued her activism and to make her own work. Engaged and committed from the outset, Gillian Wearing has deepened her relationship with Cahun's images, as expressed by new work made especially for the exhibition, such as *At Claude Cahun's grave* (cat.7). Gillian has been an inspiring collaborator. It has been a pleasure to work with such a perceptive artist, and we extend our sincere thanks to her for her vision.

Gillian Wearing and Claude Cahun: Behind the mask, another mask has relied upon many supporters, and I should first like to thank our exhibition supporters Cockayne – Grants for the Arts and the London Community Foundation, and our Spring Season sponsor Herbert Smith Freehills, as well as the generous individuals in our Exhibition Supporters Group. We are grateful to all the lenders of these precious, often unique photographs by Claude Cahun for entrusting us with their works and sharing them with our audience – and, in particular, to Jersey Heritage, keepers of the largest Cahun archive in the world, for their invaluable efforts in preserving these remarkable works. Our sincere gratitude also extends to all of the collectors of Gillian Wearing's work who have lent to the exhibition, and of course to Wearing's gallerist Maureen Paley, who has been a vital supporter from the beginning.

My sincere thanks go to the fantastic team at the Gallery: first and foremost, Sarah Howgate, Senior Curator of Contemporary Portraits, who has done an outstanding job, both in leading the exhibition and overseeing this catalogue. Sarah has been brilliantly supported by Sarah Tinsley, Director of Exhibitions and Collections; Eloise Stewart, Exhibitions Manager; Rosie Wilson, Head of Exhibitions; Ulrike Wachsmann,

Exhibitions Officer; Ian Gardner, Exhibition Designer, and Tanya Bentley, Curatorial and Administrative Assistant. I am also very grateful, as ever, to my colleagues Stuart Ager, Miranda Banfield, Pim Baxter, Robert Carr-Archer, Tarnya Cooper, Andrea Easey, Neil Evans, Richard Hallas, Daniel Isitt, Rebecca Nicholl, Phillip Prodger, Nicola Saunders, Fiona Smith, Liz Smith, Christopher Tinker, Denise Vogelsang and Helen Whiteoak. The catalogue is something of which we are very proud, and so I must also thank Dawn Ades, for contributing such an insightful essay, one that challenges the 'self-portrait' status of Cahun's work, and colleagues in the publishing team at the Gallery – Andrew Roff, Mark Lynch and Ruth Müller-Wirth – as well as designers Praline, for their sterling efforts.

Nicholas Cullinan
Director, National Portrait Gallery, London

Cat.2 *Self-portrait* from 'I am in training don't kiss me' series by Claude Cahun, c.1927

Curious spirits

Sarah Howgate

Under this mask, another mask.
I will never finish removing all these faces.[1]
Claude Cahun, 1930

You always feel that you
are the mask to some degree.[2]
Gillian Wearing, 2012

This exhibition brings together for the first time the self-portraits of French Surrealist artist Claude Cahun and British contemporary artist Gillian Wearing. Although they were born almost seventy years apart and came from different backgrounds, remarkable parallels can be drawn between the two artists. Both of them share a fascination with the self-portrait and use the self-image, through the medium of photography, to explore themes around identity and gender, which are often played out through masquerade and performance. Cahun and Wearing have many preoccupations in common, and they are associated with important art movements: Cahun with the French Surrealists and Wearing with a group of young artists who found fame in London in the early Nineties.[3] However, their trajectories as artists are markedly different. While Cahun's work was rarely published or exhibited in her lifetime, or indeed for decades after her death, Wearing has become an established artist, exhibiting internationally and winning the Turner Prize in 1997 at the age of thirty-three. Although other contemporary artists have cited Cahun as an important influence, this is the first exhibition to examine Cahun's legacy in a dialogue with the work of Wearing.[4] Developing the exhibition with Wearing has been a journey of exploration and discovery for the artist, and this catalogue charts that journey. Learning about other people and how they live their lives is at the heart of Wearing's practice. She says: 'I'm always trying to find ways of discovering things about people, and in the process discover more about myself.'[5] Wearing has not only learnt a great deal about Cahun and her work but she has also made a spiritual connection with the artist, which has resulted in the production of new 'collaborative' works for the exhibition.

Claude Cahun is born as Lucy Schwob in 1894 in Nantes, western France, into a Jewish middle-class, intellectual family. Cahun has one sibling, a brother, Georges. Her uncle is the Symbolist writer Marcel Schwob, and the arts are a way of life for her from an early age. She has a rarefied, anglophile upbringing and for a time attends English boarding school. As a teenager Cahun meets her lifelong partner and artistic collaborator, Suzanne Malherbe (fig.1), in what she describes as a 'thunderbolt encounter'. Malherbe later becomes her stepsister when Cahun's father marries Malherbe's widowed mother. The couple adopt gender-neutral names, with Malherbe becoming Marcel Moore, and move to Paris, where Cahun studies literature and philosophy at the Sorbonne. Cahun is one of the few women to be actively engaged in the Surrealist movement in the city and is involved with two Surrealist exhibitions in Paris and London. The founding Surrealist, André Breton, whom she befriends in 1932, refers to Cahun in a letter to her as 'one of the most curious spirits of our time'.[6] Cahun and Moore become increasingly involved in politics, protesting against the rise of Hitler and the spread of fascism in France.

Fig.1 *Marcel Moore (Suzanne Malherbe) and Claude Cahun (Lucy Schwob) reflected in mirror*, c.1920

Fig.2 *Self-portrait reflected in mirror* by Gillian Wearing, 1984

In 1937 Cahun and Moore move to La Rocquaise, a house in St Brelade's Bay, Jersey, where they lead a secluded life. Although they continue to be creatively active, they work in isolation, and the move marks the end of their close association with Surrealism. The couple revert to their given names, Lucy Schwob and Suzanne Malherbe, and are known by the islanders as 'les mesdames'. When the Germans invade the island in 1940 they decide to stay. They produce counter-propaganda tracts in active resistance to the Occupation, and in July 1944 they are found out, arrested, stand trial, and, briefly, are sentenced to death. The couple are imprisoned in separate cells for almost a year before Liberation in May 1945, but, although they remain defiant, prison takes its toll. They return to reclaim La Rocquaise, which had been seized by the Germans, to find that most of Cahun's work has been destroyed. In 1951 the artist receives the Medal of French Gratitude for her acts of resistance during the Second World War, and two years later Cahun makes her final visit to Paris, when she meets Breton again. Suffering increasingly from ill health, she dies in 1954 at the age of sixty. Moore dies eighteen years later, in 1972.

Cahun's biography is as complex as the artist is enigmatic. Although she is now celebrated for her imagery, Cahun thought of herself as a writer primarily. However, it was 'her dilettantism – a refusal to fit in, to be pinned down as "writer", "woman", "lesbian", and master her craft – that rendered Cahun a blind spot in the history of the last century'.[7] Cahun acknowledged this: 'Individualism? Narcissism? Certainly. My best characteristic, the one and only intentional fidelity I am capable of. You don't care? I'm lying anyway: I scatter myself too widely for that.'[8]

Wearing's own story and development appears, at least on the surface, to be more straightforward. Born in Birmingham in 1963, art is not in her DNA, and her artistic path evolves more slowly, almost subliminally. Moving to London in her late teens, she finds work as a junior clerk and becomes aware of her artistic sensibility in her early twenties. After attending evening classes at Sir John Cass School of Art, she does a Foundation course at Chelsea School of Art and then studies for a degree in Fine Art at Goldsmiths (fig.2). Here she is associated with Damien Hirst, Gary Hume and Michael Landy, who becomes her partner. Wearing wins the Turner Prize in 1997 for her film *60 Minute Silence* (1996) and from then on exhibits widely at venues including the Musée d'Art Moderne de la Ville de Paris (2001), the Museum of Contemporary Art, Chicago (2002–3), the Whitechapel Gallery, London (2012) and K20, Dusseldorf (2012–13). In 2007 she becomes a Life Member of the still male-dominated Royal Academy. Between 2000 and 2005 she is a Tate Trustee, and in 2011 she receives an OBE for her contribution to the arts. She receives public recognition for her art and enjoys success as an artist in a way that Cahun never did in her lifetime.

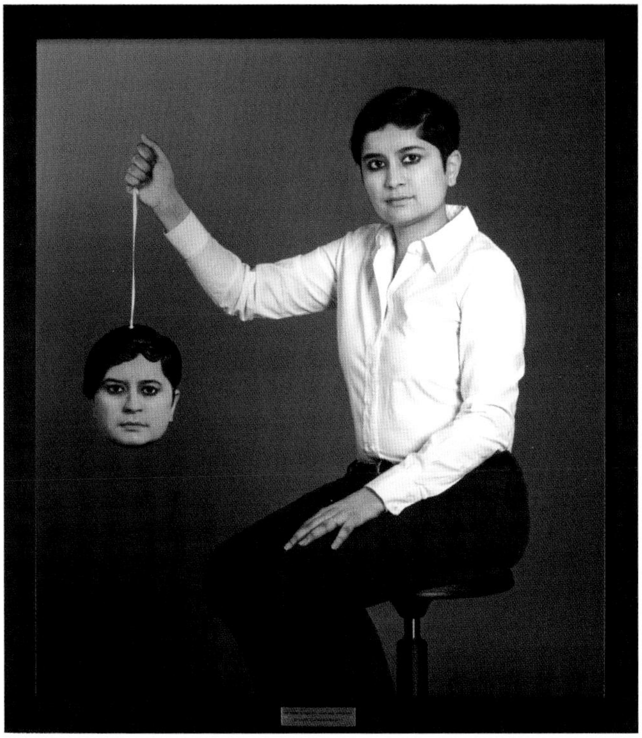

Fig.3 *Shami Chakrabarti, Baroness Chakrabarti* by Wearing, 2011.
The plaque reads: *My mask is worthy, grim and strident*.

Wearing first became aware of Cahun's photographs in the 1990s when they were rediscovered, forty years after Cahun's death in Jersey. Following the death of Suzanne Malherbe, in 1972, much of Cahun's work was put up for auction. It was acquired by John Wakeham, a book and photographs collector, who then sold it to the Jersey Heritage Trust in 1995. The publication in 1992 of François Leperlier's definitive biography, *Claude Cahun: L'écart et la métamorphose*, and subsequent exhibition, *Claude Cahun: Photographe*, at the Musée d'Art Moderne de la Ville de Paris in 1995, encouraged a growing interest in the artist's work.

For Wearing the self-portrait is central to her practice, and the National Portrait Gallery has been following her work with great interest for some time. In 2011 the Gallery commissioned the artist to create a portrait of Shami Chakrabarti (fig.3), the human-rights lawyer, campaigner and former director of the British civil liberties advocacy organisation Liberty, for the Collection. In collaboration with Chakrabarti, a public figure criticised for her mask-like 'worthy' face, Wearing arranged for her sitter to hold a mask of a more severe version of herself. The starting point for the present exhibition was a self-portrait by Wearing that uses two masks to create two different personas. Made the year after the portrait of Chakrabarti, *Me as Cahun holding a mask of my face* (2012, cat.6), is an hommage to Claude Cahun's iconic self-portrait dating from c.1927 (cat.5). It is interesting to note how Wearing's own self-portrait both differs from and resembles that of Cahun. In conversation about the Cahun work, Wearing has said:

> *But it's good to have difference; I don't want to be too similar. We were born in different times, we have different concerns, and we come from different backgrounds. She didn't know me, yet I know her. I have paid homage to her in the photographs and acknowledged her presence and the fact that we do have a spiritual camaraderie, which I would like to explore further.*

In Cahun's original work, one of several variants (cats 2–5), the artist poses provocatively as a strongman, looking out coquettishly at the viewer. She wears a white leotard emblazoned with the words: I AM IN TRAINING DONT KISS ME. Like most of her images it is sexually ambiguous – although flat-chested, she wears pasted-on nipples, and appears to be both masculine and feminine at the same time, which is exactly what Cahun considered herself to be. She has slicked-down hair with kiss-curls, pouting Clara Bow lips and love hearts painted on to her cheeks. The artist holds weights, one of which is decorated with the names of Totor and Popol, two popular comic heroes of the time. In *Me as Cahun holding a mask of my face* (2012), Wearing chooses to abandon the weights, replacing them with a different attribute – in her right hand she holds a mask of her own face suspended from a thin stick, while over her actual

Cats 3–4 *Self-portraits* from 'I am in training don't kiss me' series by Claude Cahun, c.1927

I AM IN TRAINING DONT KISS ME
TOTOR et POPOL

← Cat.5 *Self-portrait* from 'I am in training don't kiss me' series by Claude Cahun, c.1927

↑ Cat.6 *Me as Cahun holding a mask of my face* by Gillian Wearing, 2012

Fig.4 *Me as Weegee* by Gillian Wearing, 2013

face she wears a mask of Cahun. In this image she represents herself both as an artist and as Cahun. Although the kiss-curls, pouting lips and love hearts remain, the nipples are gone. Wearing's Cahun is less flat chested – this seems to be an altogether more feminine image. The head position is not mimetic – it is less tilted, and she faces the camera more directly.

On 14 November 2015, Wearing and I travelled to Jersey to view the work of Claude Cahun at the Jersey Heritage Archive in St Helier. The Archive holds the largest collection of Cahun's work in the world. It was the week after the terrorist attacks on Paris, the city Claude Cahun fled to find what she had hoped, but proved not to be, a safer haven in Jersey. At the Archive, with the help of curator Louise Downie, we had the privilege of examining in forensic detail Cahun's exquisite silver gelatin prints and negatives. In looking at Cahun's self-portraits as a body of work, shared themes began to emerge in the artists' practice. These connections have formed the basis for the development of the structure of the catalogue and exhibition. There are differences, too; in the catalogue we are able to show the artists' work side by side. These fascinating juxtapositions occur less frequently in the exhibition, in part because of the aesthetic disparities between a vintage and a contemporary print. There is also the visual challenge of variations in scale – the Cahun photographs are small and jewel-like, whereas the Wearings are more than ten times larger.

This book begins by looking at Claude Cahun's early work and her extraordinary transformation from young woman to short-haired boy to a gender-neutral figure – the Buddha and the dandy being just two of her multiple selves. Alongside Cahun's transformation, we explore Wearing's own early self-portraits – a series of recently reassessed Polaroids, taken in the late 1980s and 1990s, which she considers a precursor to the 'selfie'. We also explore Wearing's own creative evolution and the artists who have influenced her. Weegee (fig.4), Arbus (cat.51) and Warhol (cat.52) are among those into whose skin she has stepped for her self-portraits. Cahun was effectively written out of Surrealist history and only recently has this serious omission been redressed. Cahun in the context of Surrealism is explored in the next section and also in an essay by the academic Dawn Ades. For Wearing, too, Surrealism was an important early influence, although it was not a movement that was taught when she was at art school. Beyond Surrealism, Wearing has explored the temporal in her work, particularly in her 'Family Album' series (2003–6). The next sections look at masquerade and performance, playful themes that both artists develop in their work. Cahun's late self-portraits produced after the Liberation, which can be seen as *memento mori*, are explored in the final part of the catalogue. Some of these images were taken against the backdrop of the churchyard, next to the house where she was buried. In recent years Wearing has also begun producing *memento mori,* which examine the ageing process, using digital technology to predict how she might look at seventy. The final section also includes Wearing's 'collaborations' with Cahun. On the second day of our research visit to Jersey, I witnessed the early stages of one of these 'collaborative' performances. It took place in the churchyard of St Brelade's, where Cahun was buried in 1954 and, later, Marcel Moore alongside her. After a day spent poring over Cahun images in the Archive, Wearing had had some thoughts about how she might re-enact one of Cahun's late works, *Self-portrait (with masked face and graveyard)* (c.1947, cat.81). In this work Cahun presents herself like an angel, in diaphanous clothing. The setting is the garden of La Rocquaise, with the churchyard visible in the distance. The mask she holds over her face is hauntingly featureless, almost like a bee-keeper's mask. Although Cahun made this work seven years before her death, she was already suffering from ill health. This is a prescient image, with a sense of foreboding.

Dressed in a white sweater, Wearing combs her long, dark, straight hair forward over her face to form a curtain. Although the church groundsman is at work close by, she positions herself behind the shared tombstone of Cahun and Moore (fig.5), without any apparent self-consciousness. It is a Jewish grave, situated in the corner of the churchyard, and they are buried as Lucy Schwob and Suzanne Malherbe. The epitaph engraved on their tombstone reads: 'And I saw new heavens and a new earth'.[9] In the Jewish tradition, visitors have paid their respects by leaving stones as tributes around the top of the tombstone. Under Wearing's direction, I take a series of digital photographs of her adopting various poses. In some she cups her hands around her face (cat.7), as Cahun did in the original photograph. In others she is more playful and performative, wrapping her arms around the tombstone. She adopts some thirty different poses. I am sure Claude Cahun would have approved of this 'collaboration'; an attempt to peel back the layers of this most enigmatic artist more than sixty years after her death.

Fig.5 The gravestone of Cahun and Moore in St Brelade's Bay, Jersey. Photo by Gillian Wearing, 2016

1 Claude Cahun, *Disavowals or Cancelled Confessions* (Tate, London, 2007), p.183. The quotation is written in French on the photomontage *I.O.U. (Self-pride)* (1930, cat.29). See also note 5, p.59.

2 'Gillian Wearing, "I've always been a bit of a listener"', Tim Adams, *Observer*, Sunday, 4 March 2012.

3 The media referred to the group as the Young British Artists (YBAs). Wearing and her contemporaries have rejected this term, which they see as a media invention.

4 Cahun has been linked to several contemporary artists and has a dedicated following among art historians and critics working from postmodern, feminist and queer theoretical perspectives. In 1986, the American art critic Hal Foster described Cahun as 'a Cindy Sherman avant la lettre' (Jersey Heritage Trust website). *Magic Mirror,* an exhibition of April–June 2015 at the Nunnery Gallery, London, focused on contemporary British artist-filmmaker Sarah Pucill in dialogue with Claude Cahun.

5 Gillian Wearing, 'Sign Language', *Dazed & Confused*, no.25, December 1996, pp.52–5, esp. p.55.

6 André Breton wrote in a letter to Claude Cahun, dated 21 September 1938: *Vous savez très bien que vous êtes un des esprits les plus curieux de ce temps (des 4 ou 5) mais vous vous taisez à plaisir.* (You know very well that I think that you are one of the most curious minds/spirits of this time (one of four or five people) but you willingly keep quiet.)

7 'Claude Cahun: Finding a Lost Great', Gavin James Bower, *Guardian*, Tuesday, 14 February 2012.

8 *Disavowals or Cancelled Confessions*, op. cit., p.9.

9 Revelation, 21:1. The actual quote from Revelation is 'And I saw a new heaven and a new earth'.

Cat. 7 *At Claude Cahun's grave* by Gillian Wearing, 2015

I

Transformation

Claude Cahun

Self-portrait (as a young girl) (1914, cat.8) is one of the earliest extant examples of a Cahun self-portrait. In common with the majority of self-portraits produced in her lifetime the likelihood is that, although the concept was Cahun's, the photograph was taken by her partner, Marcel Moore. Photographed from above, lying on a pillow, Cahun stares directly at the photographer or viewer. The image exists in negative and print form, with the negative revealing a wider shot and a hand-drawn rectangle to indicate the crop that was made for the final print. In this symmetrical composition Cahun's head, with her wild hair, Medusa-like, spread out across the pillow, appears disembodied, as though she's floating above the sheets. The young artist has a haunted look, older than her years. Between the ages of fifteen and eighteen she had displayed suicidal tendencies and was diagnosed with anorexia. Perhaps this image, in which she looks like an invalid in a hospital bed, references these periods of ill health.

The following year Cahun's literary career was already under way when she created *Self-portrait (reading, with* L'Image de la femme*) (*The image of woman*)* (1915, cat.9). In 1914 she had enrolled in a literature and philosophy course at the Sorbonne, and her first article, 'Vues et visions', was published in a French literary magazine. In the same year she wrote the semi-biographical text 'Les Jeux uraniens', using the pseudonym Claude Cahun for the first time.[1] The serious, academic mood of this self-portrait contrasts with the more playful photographs Gillian Wearing has described taking with her friends at a similar age. The image shows Cahun in her early twenties seated at a desk, dressed in a sailor suit. On the desk are two large tomes, one of which is clearly titled *L'Image de la femme*.[2] A box camera sits on the desk beside Cahun. It is with this camera that Cahun and Moore would go on to challenge the female stereotypes highlighted in the book and create their own responses. Unlike Wearing's *Me as an artist in 1984* (2014, cat.23), in which Wearing re-enacts a photograph of herself at twenty-one, before she was fully aware of her own destiny, Cahun at a similar age appears to have a clear sense of who she is and where she is going. *Self-portrait (reading, with* L'Image de la femme*) (*The image of woman*)* is a conscious performance on Cahun's part, and the image reveals both her love of literature and interest in photography at a formative age. The sailor suit she wears also hints at the androgynous figure she is to become. Although the sailor dress became a popular mode of dress for young girls around this time, Cahun wears the sailor suit that was more popular with boys. Some years later, she was to make another self-portrait wearing a sailor suit. In *Self-portrait (in sailor hat)* (c.1920, fig.6) both the outfit and the stance contribute to making this an unequivocally male portrait.

The guise Cahun adopts in both *Self-portrait (in turban)* (1913, cat.11) and the tableau scene, *Self-portrait (in an Orientalist setting)* (1916, cat.10), suggests that she may have been influenced by her Orientalist great-uncle, Léon Cahun. In *Self-portrait (in turban)* Cahun wears a turban with a jewelled ornament on her forehead and strings of beads around her neck, projecting an exotic and feminine image. Cahun has been compared in this self-portrait to the beautiful dancer and courtesan Cléo de Mérode, who was popular at the time.[3]

In *Self-portrait (seated on granite rocks)* (c.1915–17, cat.13), Cahun has cropped her long hair so that she looks like a young boy. In this early example of Cahun using the beach as a backdrop for her portraits, she looks out at the photographer, who was probably Moore. Her partner's presence is felt in the form of her shadow in the bottom right-hand corner of the photograph. In *Self-portrait (hand on breast)* (c.1916, cat.12), Cahun adopts a more mannered, classical pose. The robe she wears has a Grecian appearance, and her skin looks bronzed, either by the sun or the use of make-up. Again she uses a stone wall on the beach as a backdrop. Her head and gaze are directed downwards, suggesting a moment of reflection.

Self-portrait (against granite wall) (1916, cat.14) is one of the first examples of Cahun's transformation into a gender-neutral figure. She wears a masculine shirt and braces. Her shaved head emphasises the symmetry and beauty of her face, as well as creating a politically charged androgynous look. Her gaze is internalised and not directed at the viewer. *Self-portrait (plaited fringe)* (1917, cat.16) in which Cahun holds her right arm above her head, reveals a more self-conscious pose. The inclusion of a constructed backdrop is a new development in her work, although the cloth appears makeshift. Cahun's hair is slightly longer than in *Self-portrait (against granite wall)*, and her headdress creates a more feminine appearance.

Self-portrait (seated cross-legged on beach) (1923, cat.17) is an example of Cahun's early experiments with the performative in an outdoor setting, in this case the beach, a backdrop she revisits in later works. Cahun and Moore spent time at the harbour town of Le Croisic in western France and on the beaches of Jersey, and the setting for this portrait is likely to be one of those locations. The artist adopts a fluid pose that is almost balletic. The sculptural form of her head is delineated by a swimming cap, which contributes to her androgynous appearance.

In *Self-portrait (shaved head, material draped across body)* (c.1920, cat.15), Cahun, set against a dark backdrop, presents herself like a sculpted bust, defined by the black line of her top against her porcelain-white skin. The image has a contemporary feel and could almost be a portrait of the late fashion editor and muse Isabella Blow. In conversation about this work Wearing has commented: 'There's a sense in her eyes of a vulnerable interiority.'

Self-portrait (shaved head, looking over left shoulder) (cat.19) and *Self-portrait (head between hands)* (cat.18), both dating from c.1920, are more staged and stripped back than Cahun's earlier works. Her black vest, worn against her white skin, creates a monochromatic look of stark contrasts. Her distinctive profile, with her birdlike hooked nose, has been compared to that of her father, Maurice (*Self-portrait (in profile, wearing corduroy jacket)* (c.1919, cat.20) and fig.7).[4] The transformation from feminine boy to gender-neutral figure is complete. In *Self-portrait (head between hands)* it is as though she is holding a mask of her face. As Wearing comments: 'It's almost like she's in a Greek play, and she's put the head on. You can almost detach it from the body. Because the hands look real, the body looks real – but the face doesn't.'

Sarah Howgate

1 Claude is a gender-neutral forename, which can be male or female in France. Cahun was the surname of her paternal uncle, Léon, and grandmother Mathilde.

2 *L'Image de la femme* (1899) is a two-volume, illustrated publication written by Armand Dayot that includes cameo portraits of exemplary women throughout the ages, from Penelope, faithful wife of Odysseus, to Empress Eugénie, wife of Napoleon III and last empress consort of France.

3 Abigail Solomon-Godeau, 'The Equivocal "I": Claude Cahun as Lesbian Subject' in *Inverted Odysseys: Claude Cahun, Maya Deren, Cindy Sherman*, ed. Shelley Rice (The MIT Press, Cambridge (Massachusetts) and London, 1999).

4 Louise Downie, 'Sans Nom: Claude Cahun and Marcel Moore', *Jersey Heritage Trust: Heritage Magazine*, 2005, p.9.

Cat.8 *Self-portrait (as a young girl)*, 1914, CC

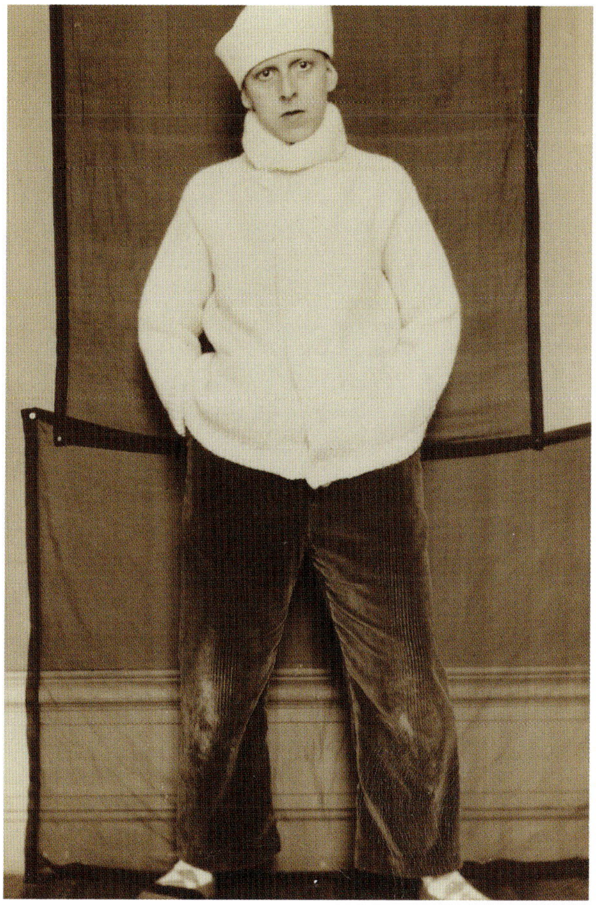

← Cat.9 *Self-portrait (reading,* L'Image de la femme*)* *(*The image of woman*)*, 1915, CC

↑ Fig.6 *Self-portrait (in sailor hat)*, c.1920, CC

← Cat.10 *Self-portrait (in an Orientalist setting)*, 1916, CC

↑ Cat.11 *Self-portrait (in turban)*, 1913, CC

← Cat.12 *Self-portrait (hand on breast)*, c.1916, CC

↑ Cat.13 *Self-portrait (seated on granite rocks)*, c.1915–17, CC

↑ Cat.14 *Self-portrait (against granite wall)*, 1916, CC

→ Cat.15 *Self-portrait (shaved head, material draped across body)*, c.1920, CC

← Cat.16 *Self-portrait (plaited fringe)*, 1917, CC

↑ Cat.17 *Self-portrait (seated cross-legged on beach)*, 1923, CC

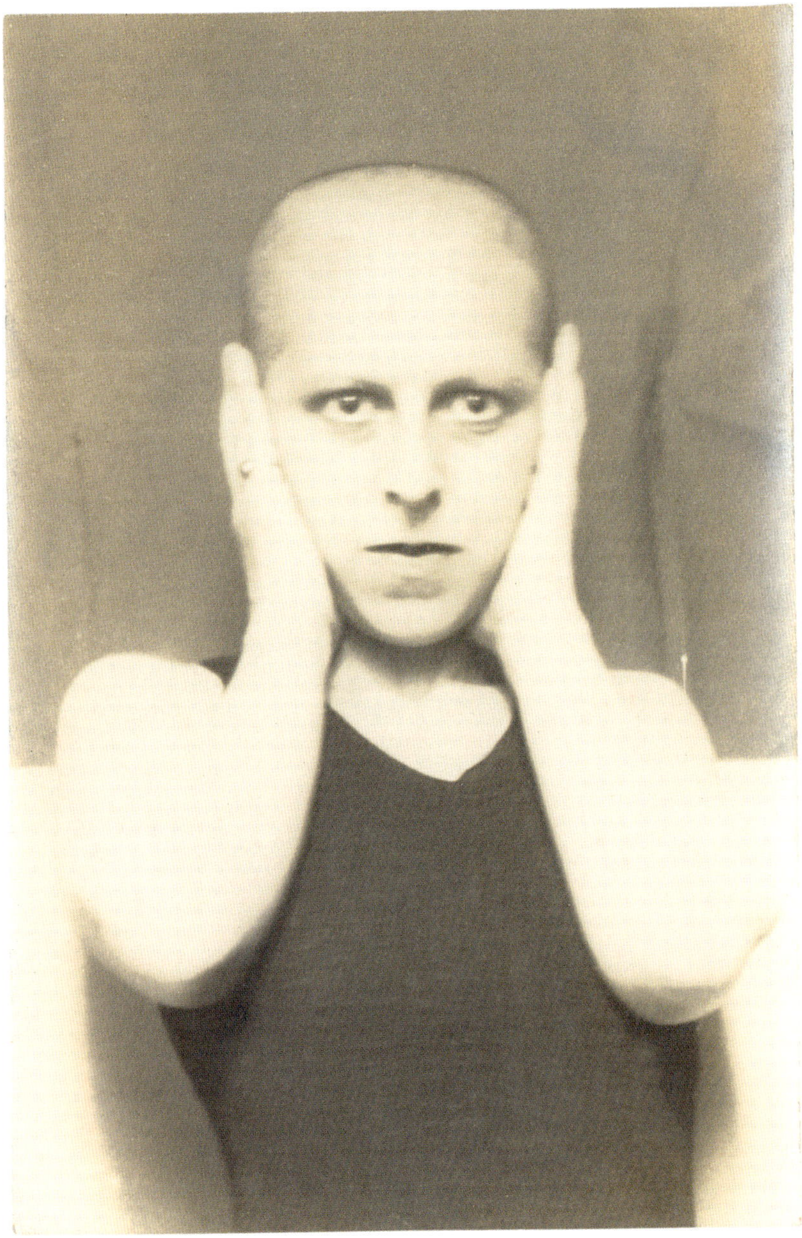

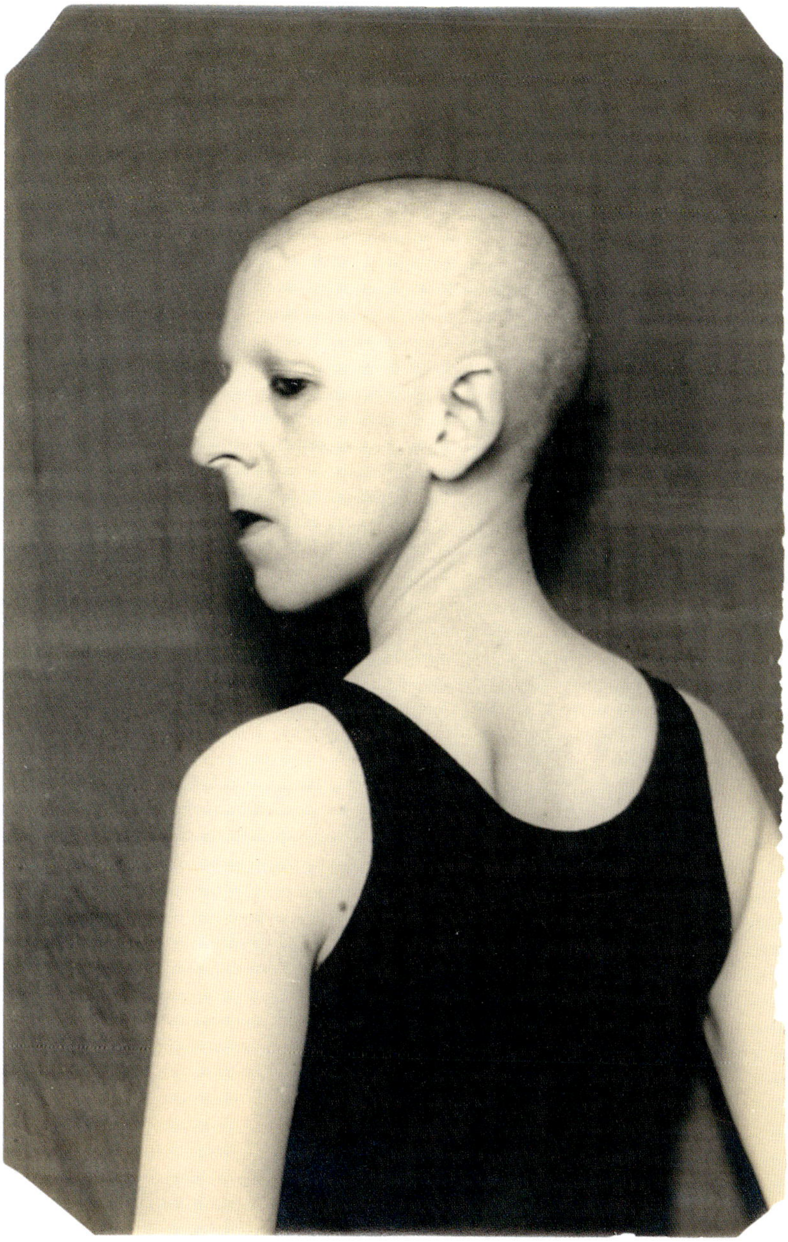

← Cat.18 *Self-portrait (head between hands)*, c.1920, CC

↑ Cat.19 *Self-portrait (shaved head, looking over left shoulder)*, c.1920, CC

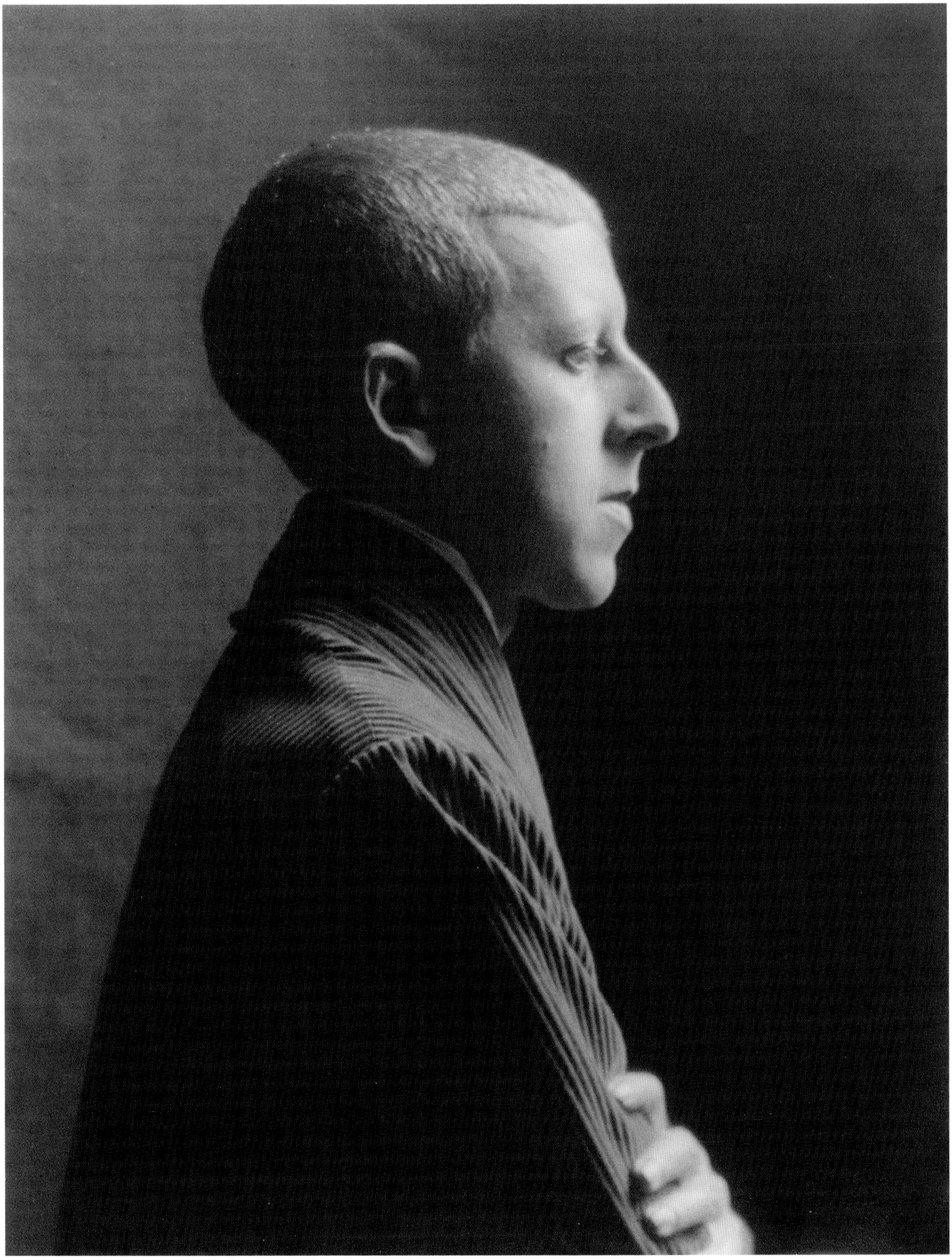

← Cat.20 *Self-portrait (in profile, wearing corduroy jacket)*, c.1919, CC

↑ Fig.7 *Maurice Schwob, Cahun's father* by an unknown photographer, 1917

II

My Polaroid years

Gillian Wearing

Although I knew the story, it was almost like I'd found someone, like a found object. Gillian Wearing, 2016

In the early 1980s, in common with many sixteen year olds, Wearing and her friends took playful photographs of each other on cheap cameras, posing as though they were on fashion shoots. At the same time, Wearing began examining her own self-image, using the more formal and private setting of the photo booth. *Self-portrait at seventeen years old* (2003, cat.21), from her 'Family Album' series, is a reconstruction of a photo-booth self-portrait from that period.[1]

Wearing created *Me as an artist in 1984* (cat.23) in 2014, thirty years after she took the original photograph on which it was based. The photograph is, therefore, a reconstruction of a self-portrait she took at the age of twenty-one, and so it marks the beginning of her evolution as an artist. Despite the title, Wearing says: 'This represents a time before I thought of myself as an artist.' However, in the tableau she is already acting out the part of an artist, surrounded by her artistic wares. She presents herself in a serious fashion with all the confidence and vanity of youth. There are signs of early artistic interests and influences: Dalí and Surrealism, figurative sculpture and mask-making. Wearing points out: 'I was trying to make sculpture and paint. I hadn't thought of photography as art at that point.' Wearing has carefully reconstructed her bedsit room in forensic detail with its damp walls and cheap furniture.

When the original photograph was taken in 1984 Wearing was doing secretarial work, while attending evening classes at Sir John Cass School of Art, where she was learning to sculpt from life. Wearing remembers:

> *When I moved to London, art continued to be something that I did in my spare time. I worked Monday to Friday, and then in the evenings or at weekends I would make art. So there was a real commitment to doing something creative, although at this point I hadn't considered becoming an artist. And then when I went to Chelsea School of Art they said I had a fine-art sensibility. And this changed the direction I thought I was heading in.*

At twenty-one, Wearing was more concerned with her own self-image than with the work she was producing. Using a mask of her younger self, she has paid a great deal of attention to her own personal style. Her face is heavily made up and indeed mask like and her hair carefully backcombed. She wears a coloured chiffon scarf and, over her monochromatic clothes, a man's brown-suede cardigan, which was considered de rigueur at the time. Wearing recalls:

> *I'm not trying to make out that I live somewhere really grand. All I care about is whether I look good. ... When you're younger your*

physical identity tends to be much more important than it is when you get older. Back then how I looked was much more important to me than it is now. I had tons of photographs of myself then – although it has diminished over the years.

In 1988, while studying Fine Art at Goldsmiths, Wearing began using the Polaroid camera to take self-portraits and continued to do so over the next decade, in intense bursts, when she could get hold of the film. By then, although she was aware of Andy Warhol's Polaroid portraits, the work she was making at college was less photography based and more sculptural. Wearing thought of the Polaroids as a private endeavour rather than an exhibition project; an artless experiment examining what she looked like.

They were for myself and no one else. … In a way, they became anthropological images because I was distancing myself from being an artist taking the photographs … I was doing something as a photographer, but in a very un-photographic way.

In total the series amounted to around 250 images (1988–2005, cat.24). Wearing became fascinated by how they documented her own age progression, in the same way that the television documentary *Seven Up!* (1964) by Michael Apted, an important influence on the artist, followed a group of seven year olds. Wearing reflects:

I wasn't thinking of the context in which I was photographing myself; I was just taking the photographs to see how I looked or if I could change or adapt my look. After a few years I realised those photographs had become a document; it was about all those incremental changes that happen in your face or attitude.

Wearing's approach to the Polaroid shoot was not scientific or formal in any way. Poses are mainly head and shoulders, mostly full frontal, but sometimes shot from below, looking up. Wearing often adopts an enigmatic expression, occasionally allowing a trace of a smile. Sometimes her arm is outstretched to take the Polaroid; at other times the camera is balanced on the end of a makeshift prop, made from a piece of driftwood or a coathanger, to create the distance she needs. Shots are taken from a distance and close up, still and in movement, brightly lit and in shadow. One of the fascinating aspects of the series is the casual backgrounds, which reveal the everyday detritus of life: a radiator, a clothes rail or a dated, boxy-looking computer. Subtle changes in Wearing's hairstyle, from long hair to bob and from signature long fringe to short fringe to layered fringe to fringe grown out altogether, mark the passage of time. The mood ranges from the self-consciously performative extrovert – Wearing heavily made up with a Warhol-style 1970s wig – to the ordinariness of her sitting with a suntan post-holiday.

A selection of the Polaroids was published as a group in the *Observer* in 1998, but they were never exhibited. Wearing stored them away in boxes, and it was only in late 2015, with the development of the National Portrait Gallery exhibition, that she reacquainted herself with them. Laying out the Polaroids on her studio floor, she was able to look at them objectively, with the distance of time. Describing them as early 'selfies', the artist recalls the addictive quality of the medium; how, at the time, she enjoyed the privacy of being able to develop them herself without having to take them to be processed. Rather like Claude Cahun's own work, which had also been stored away in boxes for decades, when Wearing returned to look at the Polaroid self-portraits, it was as though they were portraits of someone else. In 2016 she said:

> *I was presenting myself in a lot of the images unaware of the mess in my room or the location I was shooting in. This unawareness was one of the reasons I became interested in looking at the photographs again. I was looking at myself as though I was studying someone else. I rediscovered all these images and was trying to decipher who this person was. There is a similarity in my posing and the poses of a lot of young women you now find on Instagram and Twitter, etc.*[2]

Sarah Howgate

1 Before the digital age, the photo booth reflected the subject in a large screen, set against a simple colour backdrop, thereby allowing the sitter to concentrate on the pose without having to simultaneously press the shutter.

2 Quotation from Gillian Wearing in Tanya Bonakdar Gallery press release for *My Polaroid Years*, ADAA The Art Show, New York, 2–6 March 2016.

Cat.21 *Self-portrait at seventeen years old*, 2003, GW

← Cat.22 *Self-portrait*, 1985, GW

↑ Cat.23 *Me as an artist in 1984*, 2014, GW

DEC
88

1989

1991

Cat.24 A selection of Polaroids from *My Polaroid years*, 1988–2005, GW

Cat.24 continued. Installation shot from the exhibition *My Polaroid Years* at ADAA, Park Avenue Armory, New York, March 2016

III

Surrealism

Gillian Wearing and Claude Cahun

In 1922, Cahun and Moore left their home town of Nantes and moved to Paris, where the couple became involved in the artistic and intellectual life of the city. In 1925 Cahun published *Héroïnes*, a collection of feminist monologues by fairy-tale and biblical heroines.[1] In 1929, Cahun translated, into French, *Woman in Society* by the British physician and social reformer Havelock Ellis, whose controversial theories introduced the possibility of a third sex.[2] The following year Cahun was commissioned to write an autobiography but instead published her anti-memoir, *Aveux non avenus* (cat.25). In 1932, Cahun met the founding Surrealist André Breton and they became close friends. However, their relationship was complex – when she and Moore arrived at his favourite café, he would dramatically leave (page 182). Although Cahun was one of the few women who actively participated in Surrealism during its most vibrant years in the city, she was regarded as an outsider on the literary scene. Cahun became increasingly involved in politics, and in 1935 she joined Breton's left-leaning group, Contre-attaque, to protest against the rise of Hitler and the spread of fascism in France. Alongside her political activity she continued to make work and was involved in Surrealist exhibitions in Paris and London.

Whereas the majority of Surrealists were men, in whose images women appear as eroticised objects, Cahun's self-portraits explore female identity as constructed and multifaceted. *Studies for a keepsake* (1925, cat.26) is a series of four self-portraits that depict Cahun's disembodied head floating like a specimen in different poses, trapped or enclosed within a glass bell jar. At the time she made this work, Cahun was concentrating on creating assemblages of objects and photographing them in the Surrealist tradition (see *Entre nous (Between us)* (c.1930, cat.35)). In *Studies for a keepsake* she objectifies herself; with painted lips and luxurious hair, she projects a feminine image, almost like a 1930s Hollywood screen goddess, but the jar suggests that she is trapped by her own female identity. A significant work in the telling of the artist's story, it hints 'at the locking up of the I, the precariousness of an obsessed mind' as commented by the curator and art historian Juan Vicente Aliaga.[3] Cahun is known to have inherited her mother's struggle with mental illness. Some forty years after this work was created the American poet Sylvia Plath wrote *The Bell Jar* (1963), a semi-autobiographical novel originally published under a pseudonym, which charts the female protagonist's loss of mental health. The bell jar of the title is a metaphor for her character's state of mind, struggling for breath, with fears of losing her inner self in an oppressive patriarchal society. Wearing has commented on the image:

> *It looks like it might be a double exposure or a collage that was then photographed. She looks quite different again in this image, with her delicately drawn eyebrows and her hairstyle, which was very much*

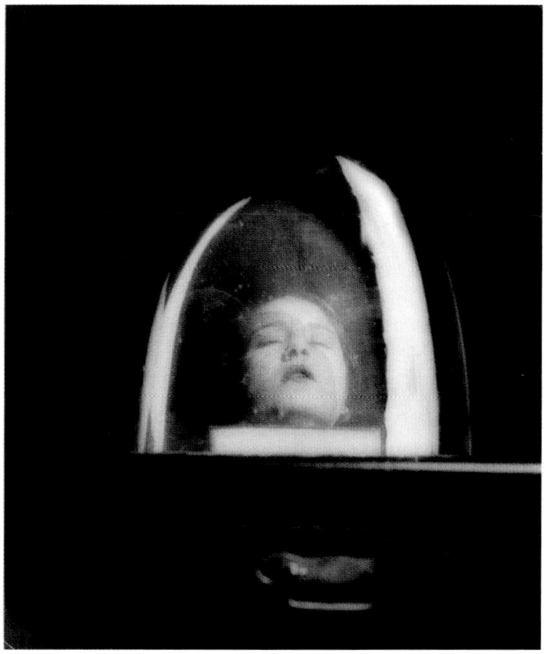

Fig.8 *Tanja Ramm under a bell jar* by Lee Miller, 1930

of its time. As there are not many images of her posing in make-up and looking feminine, her face becomes an exhibit in a claustrophobic jar. I discovered recently that Lee Miller took a photograph of the head of a woman called Tanja Ramm, also inside a bell jar [1930, fig.8].[4] *There are striking similarities – the set-up, lighting, hair and make-up are so similar, and it was taken a few years after Cahun's image. Perhaps Cahun shared her 'Keepsake' image with others.*

Cahun's double image, *Que me veux-tu? (What do you want from me?)* (1928, fig.10), fuses two earlier head-and-shoulders self-portraits. The profile image on the right is a reworking of *Self-portrait (shaved head, looking over left shoulder)* (c.1920, cat.19); the image on the left is taken from *Self-portrait (shaved head, material draped across body)* (c.1920, cat.15). This Janus-like, androgynous portrait presents two versions of Cahun's many identities; duality and mirroring are themes that run through her work. Her twin heads are severely shaved, creating an emphatic gender-neutral appearance. Wearing comments:

It's hard to tell how Claude created this image – it could be a double exposure or something achieved in the printing afterwards. But the head behind really looks as though it is in the shadow of the head in front. The double exposure only becomes obvious when you see the transparency of the shoulders. It reminds me of Cahun's statement: 'Masculine? Feminine? It depends on the situation. Neuter is the only gender that always suits me.' She was redefining gender and identity, and her photographs feel like experimental extensions of the possibilities of change. She looks like she is going to say something in the ear of her other head, confronting one aspect of herself with another. She studied philosophy at the Sorbonne and also took an interest in psychology, but this image makes me wonder how much she knew about psychoanalysis.

The frontispiece of *Aveux non avenus* (1930, cat.28) is a reproduction of a collaborative collage made by Cahun and Moore. It is a dreamlike image made up of multiple elements. On the lower left-hand side of the artwork, a glass globe is balanced on a pair of hands, held one on top of the other, as though holding a sword. Reflected in the globe are multiple enigmatic self-portraits, drawn from earlier work, of Cahun playing out different personae, with her close-cropped hair or androgynous shaved head, using masks and mirrors. The image also includes symbols created by Cahun and Moore to represent themselves – the mouth for Cahun, the writer and actor, and the eye for Moore, the artist. In the centre of the image, a pair of hands cup an eye, and a collage of a lipsticked mouth is placed playfully at the end of arms. Crowning the image are two entwined doves, perhaps a religious symbol or a reference to Cahun and Moore's relationship. In the bottom right-hand corner of the image another pair of arms are wrapped around a globe. We also see this pose in *Self-portrait (with globe)* (c.1927, fig.19). Wearing comments:

This is an enchanting image. It's an image that feels rich with metaphor. Inside one of the globes are images of Cahun's head taken from different angles. This echoes Duchamp's Five-way portrait of Marcel Duchamp, *[1917, fig.9] where a hinged mirror created five simultaneous images of him. Unlike a lot of Cahun's photographs, this is a finished piece of artwork that was produced to be seen. The collage contains elements that are similar to the original photographs, which suggests that some of the photographs Claude and Marcel took were made to be cut up and pasted to create another image.*

I.O.U. (Self-pride) (1930, cat.29) is one of ten photomontages that Cahun made in collaboration with Moore to illustrate *Aveux non avenus*. The self-pride of the title refers to 'neo-narcissism' and is Cahun's own term used to describe the subjectivity that enables her to act out alternative roles and interpersonal relationships. Included in the image are the Holy Family, representing conventional relationships, and also Russian dolls, containing the foetus in the womb at various stages of development. A stylised tree has an illustrated eye, mouth, nose, ear and hand, representing the five senses hanging from its branches. In the lower left-hand corner of the image are Cahun's head and shoulders, on top of which tower a double row of eleven overlapping faces, all growing

Fig.9 *Five-way portrait of Marcel Duchamp* by Marcel Duchamp, 1917

from the same neck. The artist's multiple selves, in which she plays out a series of cross-gendered identities, include her masculine-aviator image (see *Self-portrait (in goggles)* (1927, cat.60)) and more conventional, feminine images with painted faces. Around this phallic totem are Cahun's words: *Under this mask, another mask. I will never finish removing all these faces.*[5] In the bottom right-hand corner is an early image of Cahun as a girl from c.1915–16 together with a sexually ambiguous self-portrait from the series 'I am in training don't kiss me' (c.1927, cats 3–5).

Object (1936, fig.11) is one of Cahun's only surviving assemblages known to exist in its original form and represents the artist's exploration of the unconscious. The sculpture invites many layers of interpretation and is constructed out of a group of seemingly disparate objects: the eye, the cloud and the hand, as well as text, which relates to Cahun's political activity and foreshadows her involvement in the underground Resistance movement during the Second World War. The eye, a key Surrealist symbol of inner perception, as well as suggestive of female anatomy, is a recurring theme in Cahun's work and can also be seen in many of the collages made for *Aveux non avenus*. In the extraordinary portrait *Lucie au Kid (Lucie and Kid)* (c.1925, cat.30) Cahun poses with her cat – their eyes bear a striking resemblance to each other.

A version of the doll-like hand found in *Object* can also be found in *Untitled* (*four-hands image*) (1936, cat.32). This distinctly strange still-life is comprised of four overlapping hands: Cahun's own hands, a cast of her left hand in much darker skin tones and a tiny doll-like hand with a frill around the wrist on the end of the artist's little finger. Using dramatic lighting, Cahun creates a surreal collage of disembodied limbs, in which the hands appear to have personalities. Six years earlier, Cahun and Moore had made collages for *Aveux non avenus* by assembling images of her limbs and other parts of her body, taken from her own photographs.

Wearing shares Cahun's fascination with hands: 'There's something odd about hands; they have their own personality in a weird way. They're attractive to look at as well, unlike feet.' Unaware of Cahun's use of hand imagery at the time, Wearing created surreal life casts of her own hands. *The artist's hand* (2012, cat.31) is both a wax cast of Wearing's right hand and a play on the term used to describe an original piece of work created by an artist. The fingernails of Wearing's writing hand are painted in primary colours and black and white, the palette of Piet Mondrian, perhaps referencing her artistic sensibility. The hand is clawlike, although the object it grasps is invisible.

In 2014, Wearing created two more casts of her hands in resin, this time outstretched like Cahun's hands in the four-hands photograph of 1936. They are based on an anonymous visit to a palmist and titled *My misfortune (left)* and *My fortune (right)* (cats 33–4). The palmist's predictions are handwritten in coloured pen on different lines of fortune on the palms of her hands. The left hand, traditionally associated with the devil, contains pessimistic predictions, including 'Stay away from gossiping and do not befriend people with negativity in their lives.' The right hand features optimistic prophecies, such as 'You could certainly write a novel.' Wearing's fascination with palmistry and spiritualism is a natural extension of her interest in reality television and method acting – a play between the real world and the world of fantasy.

Je tends les bras (I extend my arms) (c.1932, cat.36) is a rare example of a Cahun work with an expressive title. As the title suggests this photograph depicts a performative pair of arms, assumed to be Cahun's, apparently emerging from a granite gatepost. The arms extend outwards with spread fingers, as though they are reaching for something or somebody. Cahun appears to be 'wearing' the rock to produce a surreal and comic effect; to create the illusion, the artist stands behind the monolith so that her body is concealed, and her left arm protrudes through a hole in the stone. The collaging of the phallic monolith and the feminine ornamented arms produces a meaning that cannot be attributed to either gender.

Cahun also created surreal, staged self-portraits using her whole body as an object on the beach and in the rock pools of St Brelade's Bay in Jersey. In *Self-portrait (naked, reclining on sand with coiled seaweed)*, (c.1930, cat.37), Cahun is lying full-length on her belly, wrapped only in stringlike seaweed, which delineates her body. She looks down on a rock pool, referencing Narcissus staring at his own reflection. In this work she is depersonalised – her face is not visible. In *Self-portrait (double exposure in a rock pool)* (c.1928, cat.38), Cahun created a mirror image of herself lying, Ophelia-like, in a rock pool, a diaphanous fabric draped around her naked body. Her face, with eyes closed, is turned towards the sun, as though worshipping it. Her waves of blonde hair create an altogether softer, more feminine persona compared to her younger, more androgynous look.

When Cahun moved to Jersey she reverted to her given name, Lucy Schwob, apart from when she communicated with the Surrealist circle. She and Moore led a secluded life on the island and had little contact with the locals. Despite their sheltered lives Cahun held on to her Surrealist sensibility. Before the Second World War the couple were visited by their old friends the poet and artist Henri Michaux and Breton's second wife, the painter Jacqueline Lamba, with her daughter, Aube. Post-Liberation and after her release from prison, Cahun reconnected with her Surrealist roots when she visited Breton in Paris in 1953, the year before her death. Breton's 'curious spirit' to the end (see page 9).

Sarah Howgate

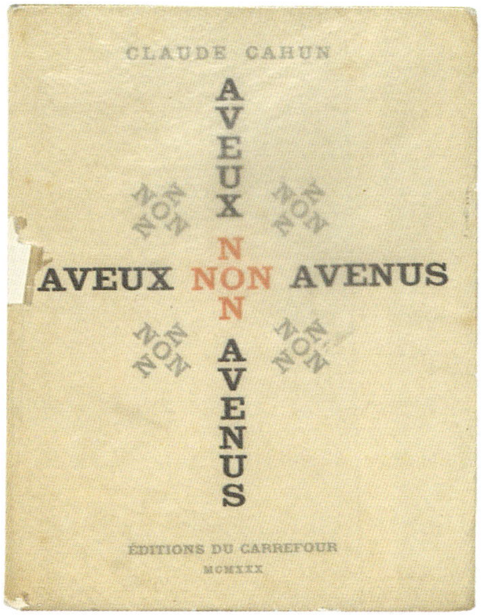

Cat.25 *Aveux non avenus* cover, 1930, CC

1 In Katharine Conley's essay, 'Claude Cahun's Counter-archival Héroïnes' in *Don't Kiss Me*, Louise Downie (Tate, London; in association with Jersey Heritage Trust, 2006), she writes that Cahun published the majority of the stories in two separate journals in 1925 (*Mercure de France*, no.639, 1 February, pp.622–43, and *Le journal littéraire*, no.45, 28 February, p.8). The whole text was only published posthumously, once found after her death in Jersey; first published in English translation in 1999 for the *Inverted Odysseys* exhibition and by her biographer François Leperlier in 2002.

2 Havelock Ellis's posited a third sex, uniting masculine and feminine traits, but existing as neither one nor the other.

3 Juan Vicente Aliaga, 'Claude Cahun Reinvented: Notes and Comments for a Biographical Cultural Visit', *Claude Cahun*, exh. cat. (Institut Valencià d'Art Modern, Valencià, 2001), p.43.

4 A painting by Man Ray, *Aline et Valcour*, 1950, uses similar imagery.

5 The French translation as written on the photomontage reads '*Sous ce masque un autre masque. Je n'en finirai pas de soulever tous ces visages.*'

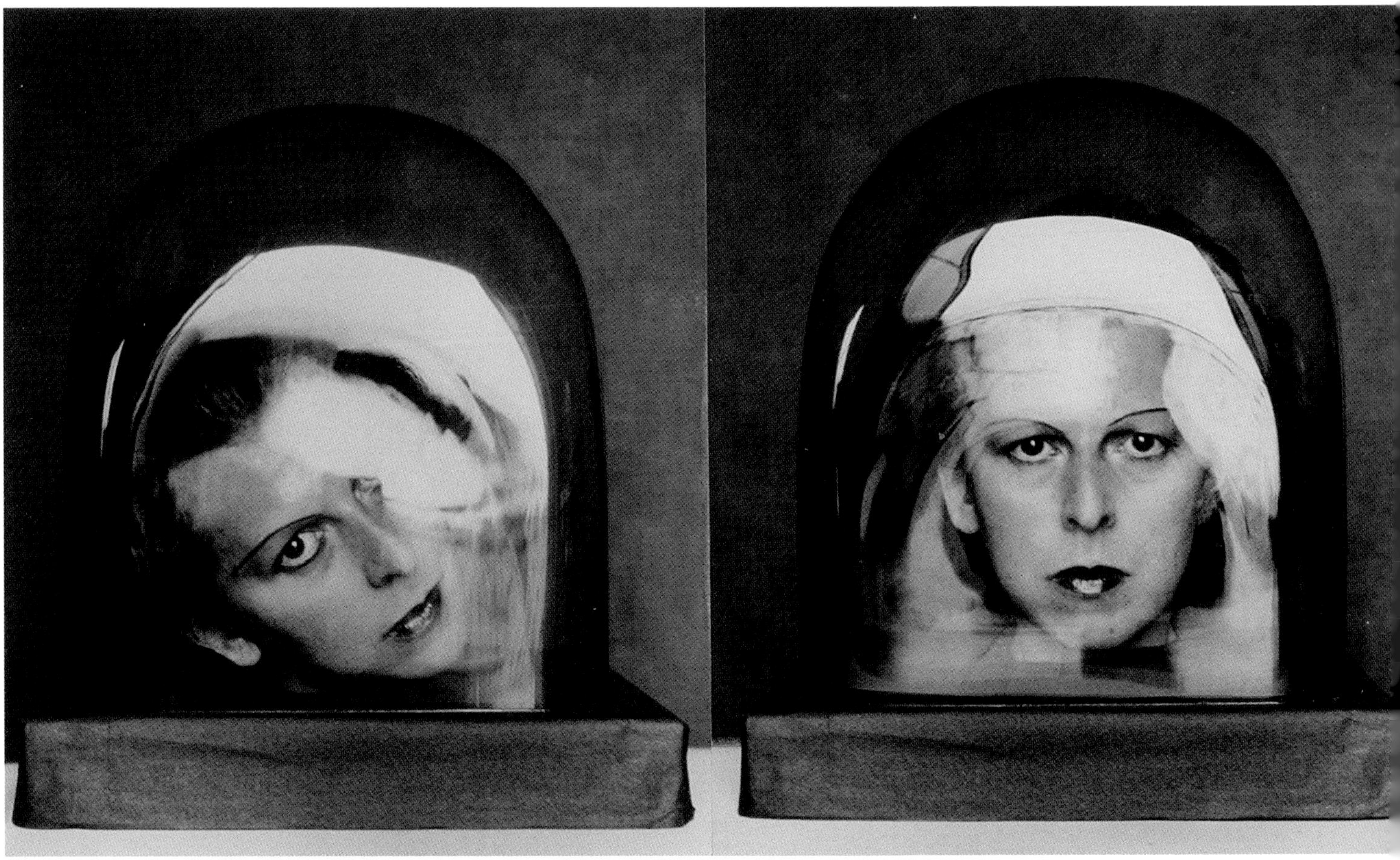

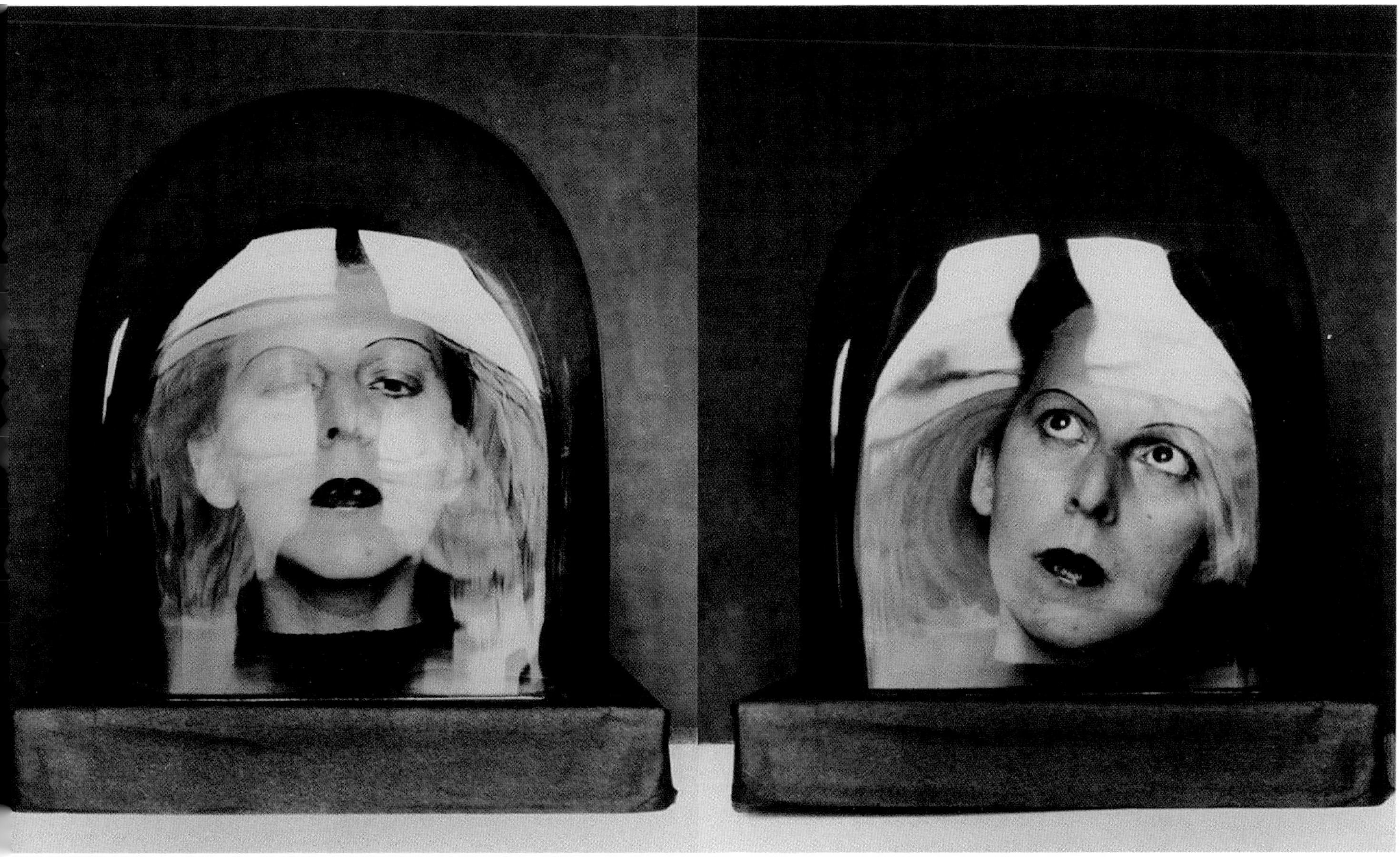

Cat.26 *Studies for a keepsake*, 1925, CC

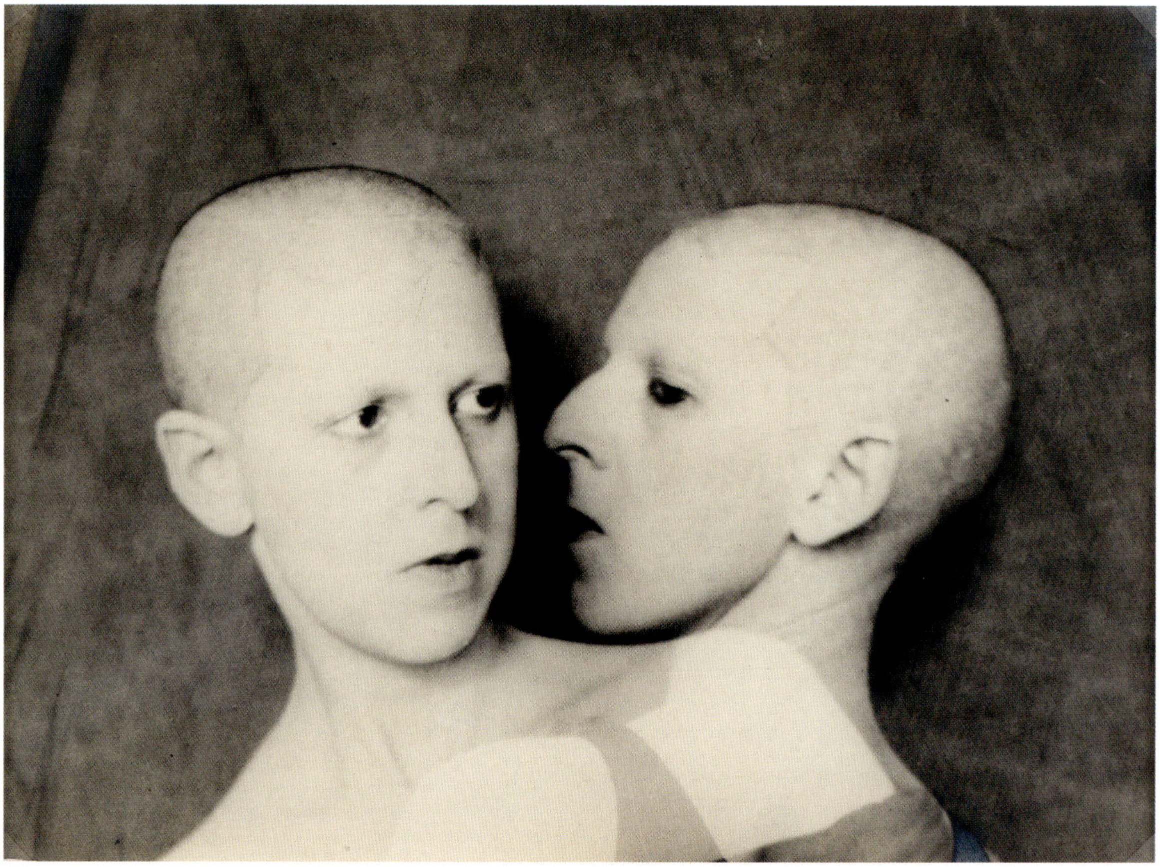

↑ Fig.10 *Que me veux-tu? (What do you want from me?)*, 1928, CC

→ Cat.27 *Aveux non avenus* photomontage prefacing chapter III *E.D.M. (Sex)*, 1930, CC and MM

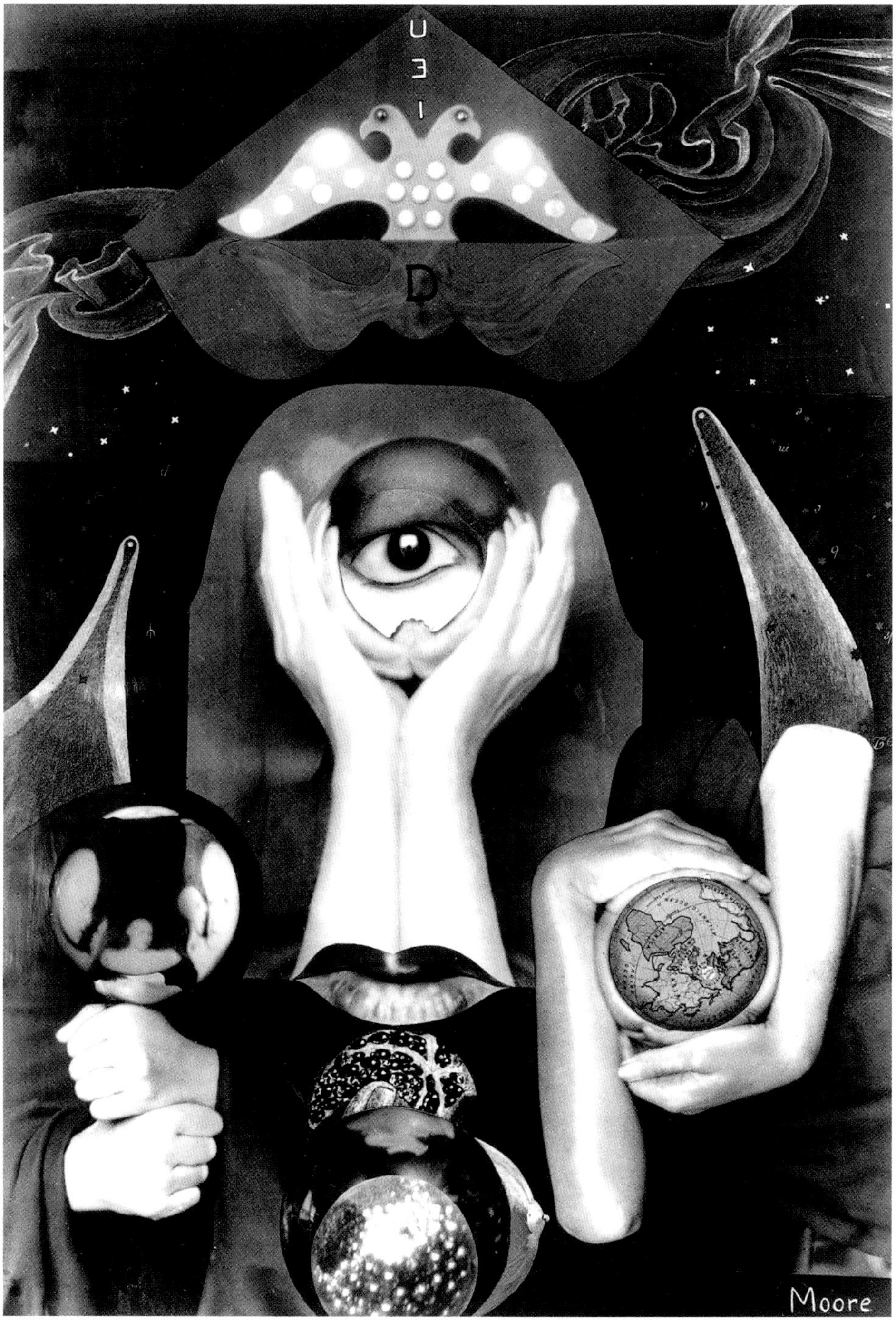
Moore

← Cat.28 *Aveux non avenus* frontispiece, 1930, CC and MM

↑ Cat.29 Photomontage prefacing chapter IX *I.O.U. (Self-pride)* from *Aveux non avenus*, 1930, CC and MM

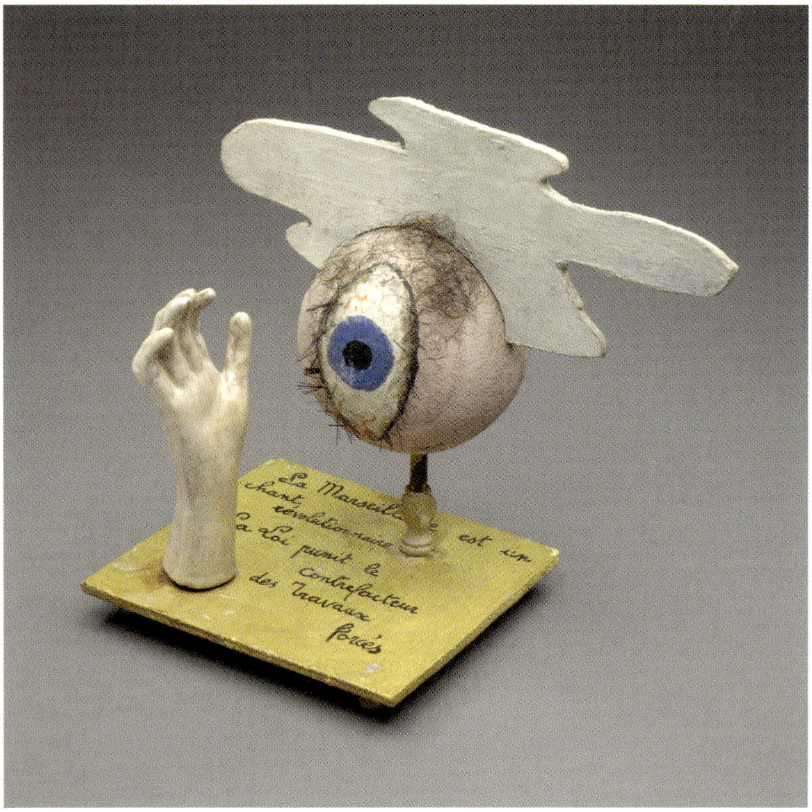

↑ Fig.11 *Object*, 1936, CC

→ Cat.30 *Lucie au Kid (Lucie and Kid)*, c.1925, CC

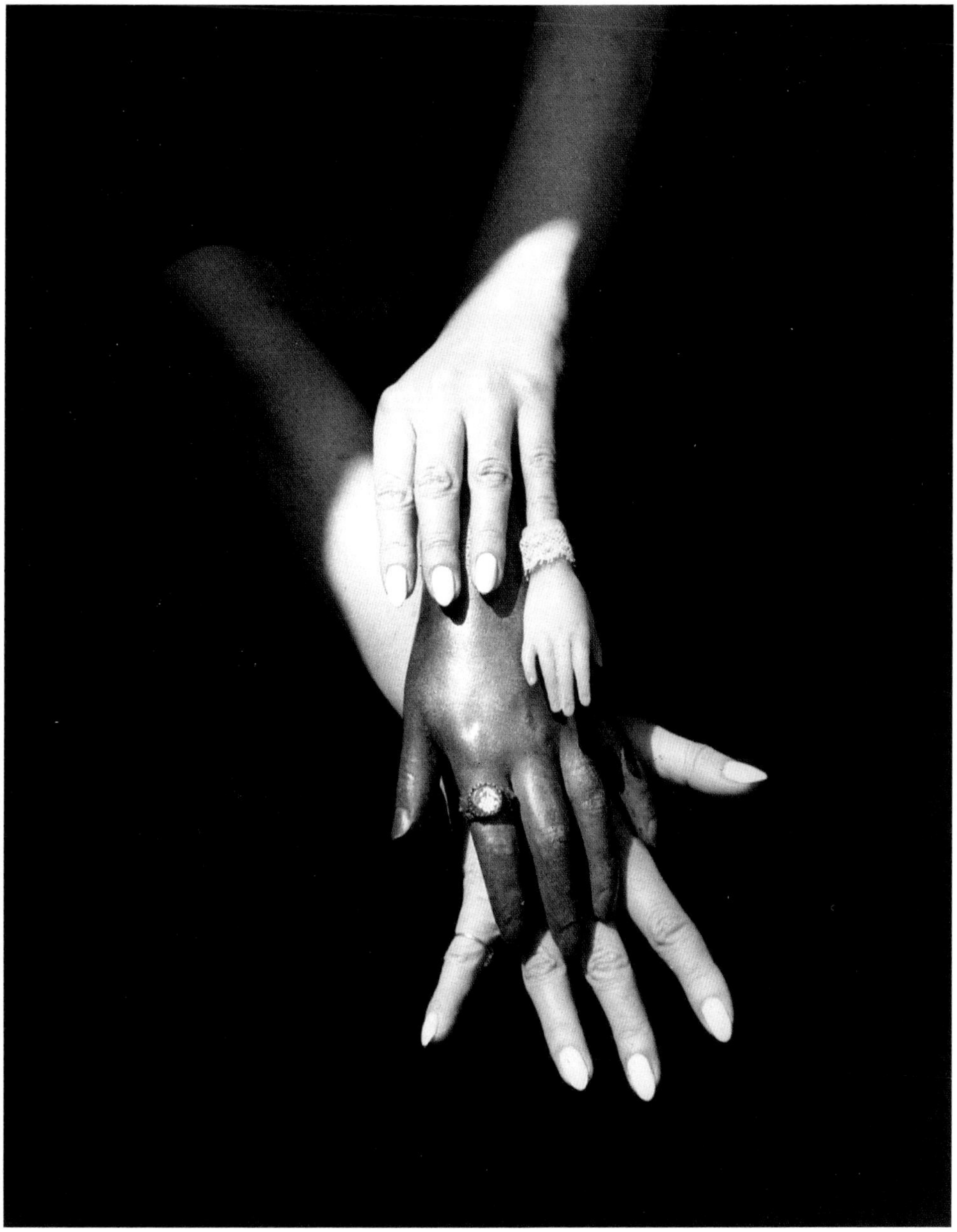

← Cat.31 *The artist's hand*, 2012, GW

↑ Cat.32 *Untitled (four-hands image)*, 1936, CC

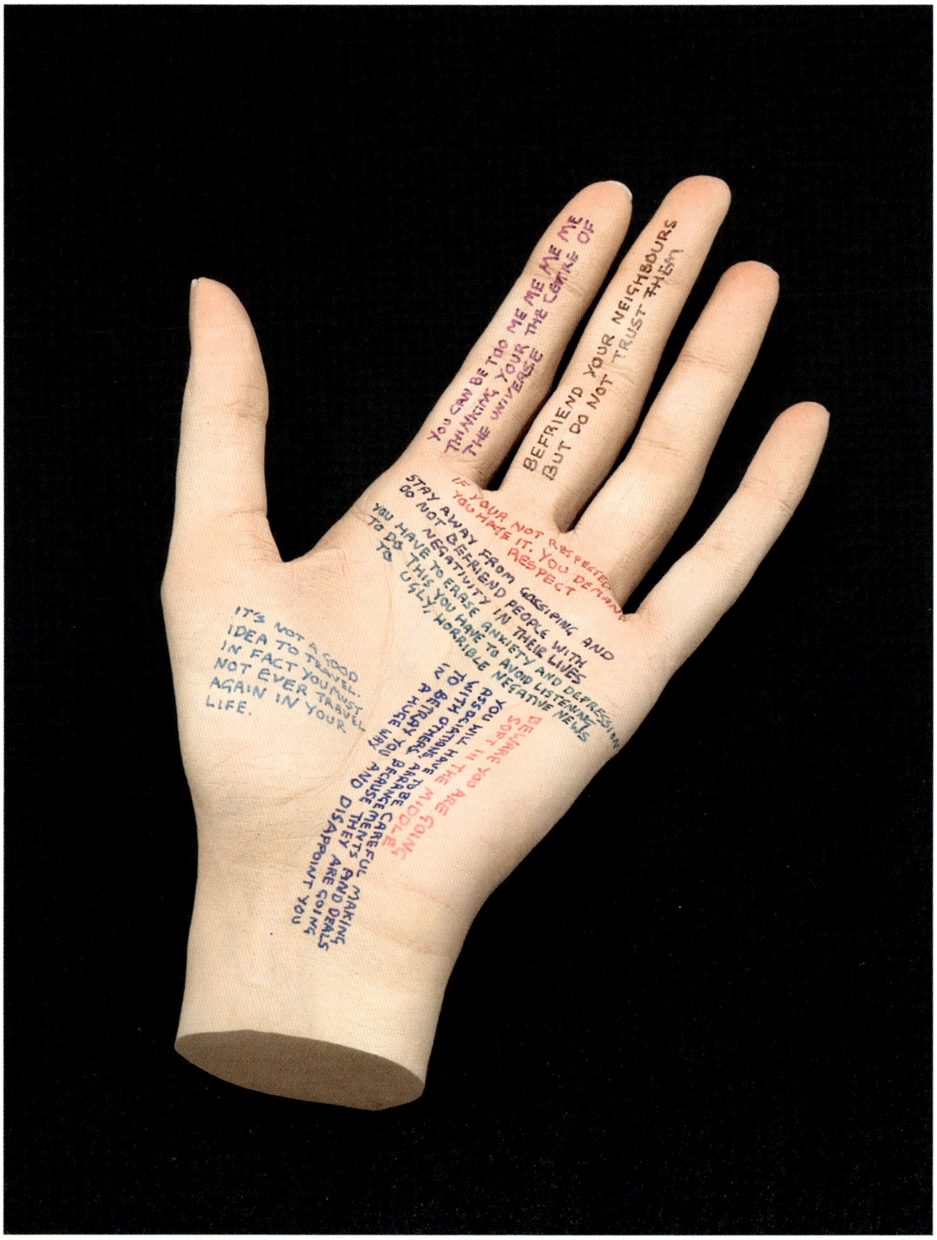
YOU CAN BE TOO ME ME ME ME
THINKING YOUR THE CENTRE OF
THE UNIVERSE
BEFRIEND YOUR NEIGHBOURS
BUT DO NOT TRUST THEM
STAY AWAY FROM GOSSIPING AND
DO NOT BEFRIEND PEOPLE WITH
NEGATIVITY IN THEIR LIVES
YOU HAVE TO ERASE ANXIETY AND DEPRESSION
TO DO THIS YOU HAVE TO AVOID LISTENING
TO UGLY, HORRIBLE NEGATIVE NEWS
IT'S NOT A GOOD
IDEA TO TRAVEL.
IN FACT YOU MUST
NOT EVER TRAVEL
AGAIN IN YOUR
LIFE.
BEWARE YOU ARE GOING
SOFT IN THE MIDDLE

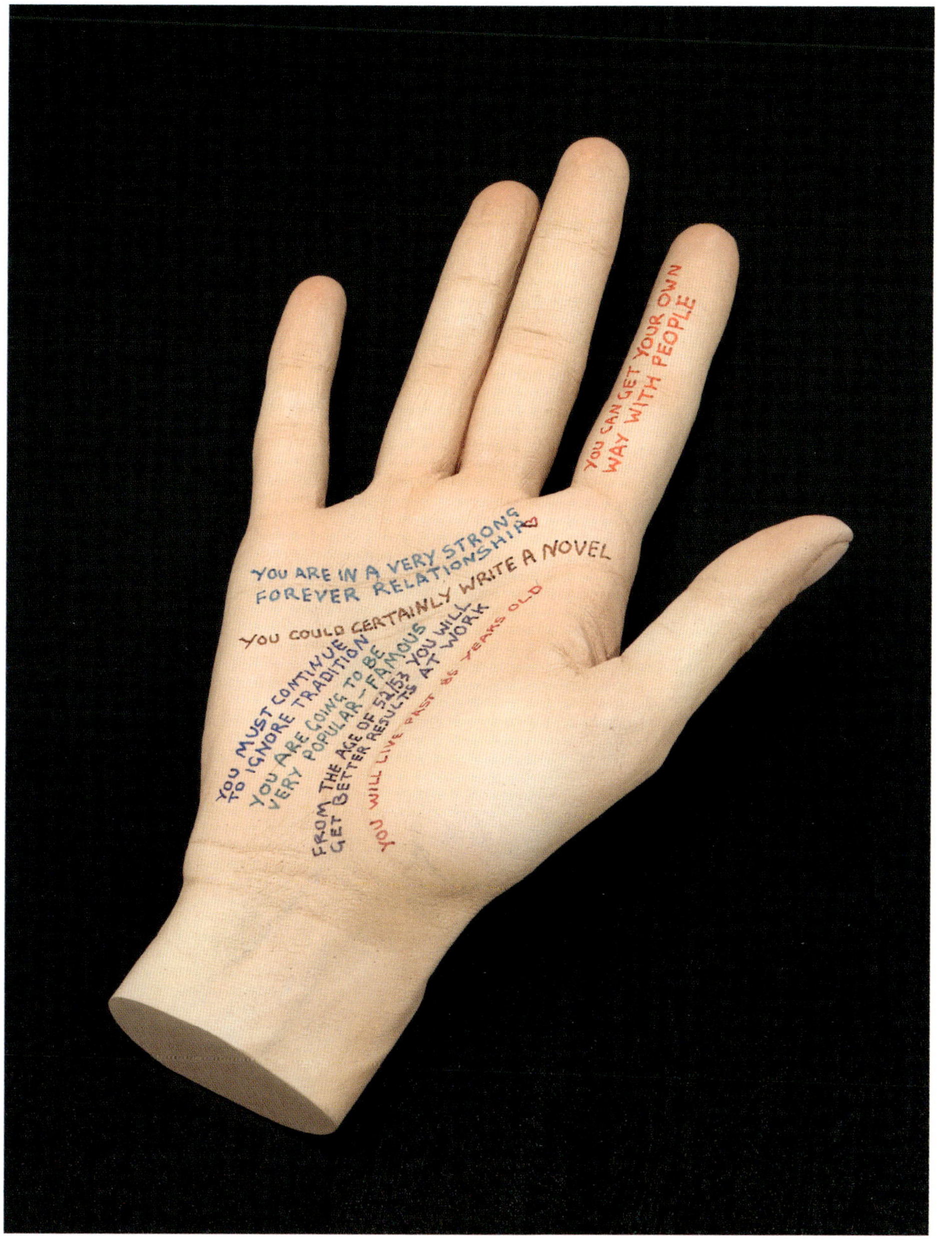

← Cat.33 *My misfortune (left)*, 2014, GW

↑ Cat.34 *My fortune (right)*, 2014, GW

← Cat.35 *Entre nous (Between us)*, c.1930, CC

↑ Cat.36 *Je tends les bras (I extend my arms)*, c.1932, CC

← Cat.37 *Self-portrait (naked, reclining on sand with coiled seaweed)*, c.1930, CC

↑ Cat.38 *Self-portrait (double exposure in a rock pool)*, c.1928, CC

IV

Transcending time

Gillian Wearing and Claude Cahun

In the 'Family Album' series, Wearing uses mimetic reproductions of old photographs to re-create herself as her own close family: her siblings, parents, uncle, grandparents and younger versions of herself aged three, seventeen and twenty-seven. Wearing plays with the notion of time in this series; in the self-portraits as her parents and grandparents she is re-creating them at an age before she knew them, before she was even born. The portraits are linked genetically – Wearing looks like her relatives, while at the same time looking like herself. Generations of Wearings merge into each other through the 'wearing' of masks.

When the 'Family Album' is reproduced in a book, on first glance, it appears quite conventional: a history of the family photograph album, from the 1950s studio portrait to the 1980s photo booth. However, when we are confronted with the actual portraits in a gallery setting, they become contemporary artworks – framed in disruptive high-key and pastel colours, the scale has shifted from the comfortably domestic to the monumental. As one spends time looking at the works, it slowly emerges that what each family portrait has in common is that Wearing's own eyes are gazing out from behind the prosthetic masks. The artist's eyes are the visual link that connects them all. Wearing commented on *Self-portrait as my mother, Jean Gregory* (2003, cat.41): 'My eyes are the only thing I have to use, but I try to make them as hopeful and young as possible.'[1]

There is a mood of optimism in Wearing's self-portraits as her parents. In the tradition of the formal photography conventions and dress of the time, they appear older than their years. However, both her mother and father look handsome and poised for exciting times ahead. Her father, in *Self-portrait as my father, Brian Wearing* (2003, cat.42), with his Brylcreemed hair and dinner suit, has film-star good looks. By including their full names in the titles, Wearing reinforces the individual identities they had before parenthood. Wearing reflected on her *Self-portrait as my mother, Jean Gregory*: 'She was this quite innocent, optimistic young woman, I think. You are trying to get that across somehow.'[2]

There is a sense that Wearing, in her role as daughter, is trying, retrospectively, to instil hope into the re-creation of her mother, in the way that parents usually do for their own children. Jean Gregory is living again through her daughter. Beneath this surface optimism is a sense of melancholy and disappointment: life didn't quite work out as the studio portraits predicted; when Wearing was a teenager, long after the original photographs were taken, her parents divorced. Her father died in 2005 while Wearing was still in the process of making the series. We don't know how this loss affected Wearing's attitude to the work, but she continued with the series, going further back in time to make the self-portraits as her grandparents in 2006.

In *Self-portrait as my grandmother, Nancy Gregory* (cat.43), and *Self-portrait as my grandfather, George Gregory* (cat.44), both 2006, Wearing's maternal grandparents exude the comfort and confidence of maturity. In reality they were much younger than they appear when the original photographs were taken; her grandfather, who died young, was only in his fifties. In 2002, Wearing created a video of her grandmother when much older, *Nancy Gregory* (cat.93), which predates these photographs of her grandparents. Rather than the proud woman wearing the fur collar in the studio photograph, Wearing's grandmother is seen slumped in a wheelchair, a poignant reminder of the sadness and indignity of old age.

Wearing's fascination with the role of inheritance doesn't appear to have been shared by Cahun. While she inherited her family's literary interests, there are few references to her family in her photographic work. There are some photographs of her father, but photographs of her mother, with whom Cahun had a difficult relationship, are rare. *Self-portrait (seated cross-legged like Buddha)* (1927, cat.46), is one exception to this, in that it is a self-portrait that references her uncle, Léon, from whom Cahun inherited an interest in Buddhism. In this work, Cahun presents herself as an androgynous figure, seated cross-legged on a mat in the lotus position. Wearing a cap, strings of beads and a golden robe, she strikes an attractive figure. Brahmin Sonadanda's description of Buddha could describe Cahun herself: 'handsome, good-looking and pleasing to the eye, with a most beautiful complexion. He has a godlike form and countenance, he is by no means unattractive'.[3] Cahun doesn't adopt the traditional *asana* of eyes closed, nor does she look down or even 'internalise' her gaze. Instead she looks directly out at the camera in a performative role as Buddha. While the position of her hands could be interpreted as a traditional *asana*, they also form the shape of an eye, a recurring motif for Cahun, which mirrors the form of the female genitals.

In *Self-portrait as my brother, Richard Wearing* (2003, cat.48), Wearing re-enacts a snapshot of her brother taken by her mother in 1990. 'It was so cool with a real feeling of the moment, of being young and getting ready for a night out,' Wearing has commented.[4] She uses his bedroom in the family home, the setting for the original photograph, in her reconstruction. This performative role was challenging for the artist as it not only involved wearing a mask but also a heavy, full body suit (fig.48). The masquerade was so successful that people questioned the image. Wearing observed: 'This is the one image that people find it hard to believe is me – some people have gone so far as to say they think I Photoshopped my eyes into old images. I do try and leave quite a bit of space around the eyes so you can see it's a mask.'[5]

As a roadie for rock bands, Richard Wearing adopts an androgynous look, with his long, dark hair, resembling his sister Gillian's. Wearing's photographs have been compared with historical paintings, and this depiction of her brother, caught in a private moment at his *toilette*, combing his hair, resonates with Edgar Degas' portraits of women doing just that (fig.12). However, Richard Wearing is surrounded by dirty washing and the general detritus of life, typical of a young man's bedroom, including a flat glass of lager on the windowsill, all of which has been carefully reconstructed by Wearing.

Cahun's *Self-portrait (as a dandy, head and shoulders)* (1921–2, cat.45) is an interesting counterpoint to this work – an interpretation of a male dandy in 1920s Paris. The Surrealists had a fascination with androgyny, and in this image Cahun adopts a distinctly male full-frontal pose and direct gaze. The artist's shaved head and clothes signify masculinity, too – a severe black jacket, white scarf and pocket handkerchief.

There are remarkable comparisons to be made between Cahun's and Wearing's re-enactments of themselves as young girls. In Cahun's *Self-portrait (in cupboard)* (c.1932, cat.49), the artist, dressed as a young girl with ankle socks and a bow in her hair, is caught sleeping, curled up in a foetal position inside a laundry cupboard, calling to mind the painter Balthus' depictions of prepubescent girls. Without the use of masks, Cahun creates the private world of a child attempting to hide from adult eyes. One possible reading of the image is that Cahun wants to return to the innocence of childhood. There are obvious references to Freud's dream therapy, too, and Oedipal myths.

Although Wearing's 'Family Album' appears on the surface to be ordinary and everyday, the series has also been linked to the Oedipus myth: 'Wearing's *Family Album* is an incestuous drama of Oedipal dimension,' writes Juliana Engberg in the 2006 exhibition catalogue *Living Proof*.[6] In Wearing's own reconstruction of her younger self, *Self-portrait at three years old* (2004, cat.50), her mature eyes peer out from the mask of an innocent, much younger face with a snub nose.

Fig.12 *Woman combing her hair*
by Edgar Degas, c.1885

There is a tension in this portrait between the gaze of experience and a young child's eyes, large and out of proportion with the other facial features. Whereas three year olds look out at the world with wonder, a mature adult, particularly an artist, has a more introspective view, and this notion is crystallised in this self-portrait, which appears to have a more cynical mood than Cahun's dreamlike version of childhood.

Wearing comments on Cahun's work *Self-portrait (in cupboard)*:

> *The image is clearly connected to psychoanalysis, dreams and age regression. It's important to recognise that there's a kind of tableau here of carefully positioned objects. This is such a key image, and we're looking at it in isolation. It does make me wonder if there weren't other similar images and maybe she tore up the rest? She couldn't have dressed up, gone to all that trouble and then just taken one photograph. She's in her thirties but seems so diminutive in the image. It feels very mysterious.*

There are interesting connections to be made between Wearing's *Self-portrait at twenty-seven years old* (2012, cat.40) and Cahun's *Self-portrait (with star-shaped pin)* (c.1930–9, cat.39). The portraits examine the artists' self-image and record their ageing process in a private yet formal space. Wearing's work is a reconstruction of a photo-booth image taken in the 1980s. Although re-created on a much larger scale, it retains the repetitive format of the photo-booth strip, with each image revealing a subtly different version of herself. Only by scrutinising the image closely does one become aware she is wearing a mask of her younger self. The duplication of Cahun's image and the directness of the head-and-shoulders pose suggest it was staged in a studio for a passport. With hindsight, it is impossible not to associate the striking star-shaped pin with the yellow-star badge that Jewish people were forced to wear in Nazi-occupied Europe.

Two years after completing the 'Family Album' series Wearing began developing a body of work devoted to her artistic or spiritual family, as she described it. The first in the large-format black-and-white 'Me as' series was her self-portrait as the American photographer Diane Arbus, titled *Me as Arbus* (2008, cat.51). Wearing's reincarnations as her other artistic heroes followed with *Me as Mapplethorpe* in 2009 (see cat.91) and *Me as Warhol in drag with scar* in 2010 (cat.52). Over time this spiritual family has expanded to tell the history of photography through its greats, from William Henry Fox Talbot to August Sander and beyond. Unlike the portraits in the 'Family Album' series, which are taken from a single snapshot or studio photograph, Wearing's homages to artists are often made up of a collage of different references.

Wearing has cited Warhol as an early formative influence, dating back to her first years in London, when she went to see his films with her friends Kimberly and Michele. *Me as Warhol in drag with scar* (2010, cat.52) looks highly believable as a portrait of the Pop artist – authentic to anyone familiar with his work. However, in reality it is a seamless conflation of two distinctive portraits: Richard Avedon's exquisite 1969 portrait of Warhol revealing his scar after he had been shot by Valerie Solanas and a portrait by Christopher Makos, from 1981, of Warhol in make-up and a Marilyn Monroe-platinum wig. The image is uncomfortable not just in its brazenness but also in its suggestion that Warhol is not this ever-youthful figure – the masculine Brando leather jacket and feminine blonde wig signify a transgender youth, but the skull-like face tells a different story. Makos's shot is an homage to Marcel Duchamp's female *alter ego* Rrose Sélavy (fig.13), a portrait familiar to Cahun, and so, in turn, the Wearing re-enactment continues the ancestral line.

Diane Arbus is a photographer with whom Wearing was less familiar when she was introduced to her work by observers, who made a comparison between Arbus's portraits and Wearing's 'Signs' series (fig.45). Like her telepathic connection with Cahun, parallels can be found in her work even before Wearing was aware of the artist. Arbus, like Wearing, had a fascination with the everyday and the extraordinary lives that lie behind the ordinary. Wearing presents Arbus as an androgynous figure in beatnik black sweater and jeans, wearing a Rolleiflex like an ornament around her neck. Unlike Wearing's Warhol self-portrait, this image is not a reconstruction of an Arbus self-portrait. Arbus's own self-portraits often featured her camera centre stage. Arbus's 1945 semi-naked self-portrait while pregnant, and double self-portrait with her baby Doon, present a more vulnerable, feminine image than Wearing's. Wearing depicts Arbus in the same way that Arbus portrayed her subjects – looking directly out at the camera, a pose that is echoed in Cahun's own self-portraits. Arbus's statement about photography as a multi-layered medium echoes Wearing's and Cahun's own thinking: 'A photograph is a secret about a secret. The more it tells you, the less you know.' [7]

Sarah Howgate

1 'Gillian Wearing, "I've always been a bit of a listener"', Tim Adams, *Observer*, Sunday, 4 March 2012.

2 Ibid.

3 Majjhima Nikaya Sutta 53.2.

4 'A Room With Your Views', University of Brighton Gallery, 30 April–29 May 2016 press release, Brighton Festival 2016.

5 Ibid.

6 'By stint of wearing face and full body masks, Wearing has become her mother, father, sister, brother and uncle, the grandparents, and has doubled herself. Her eyes – the vulnerable, Oedipal portal – indicate both a life within and a kind of weird mummification within the family body.' Juliana Engberg, *Gillian Wearing: Living Proof*, exh. cat. (Australian Centre for Contemporary Art (ACCA), Melbourne, 2006), p.20.

7 'Five Photographs by Diane Arbus', *Artforum*, vol.9, May 1971, pp.64–9.

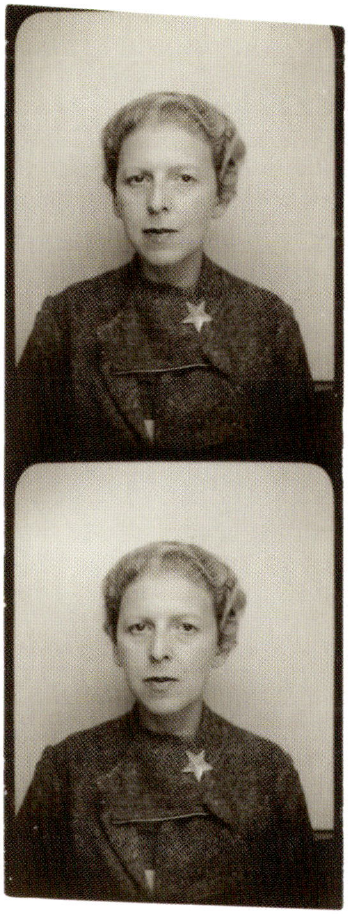

↑ Cat.39 *Self-portrait (with star-shaped pin)*, c.1930–9, CC

↗ Cat.40 *Self-portrait at twenty-seven years old*, 2012, GW

← Cat.41 *Self-portrait as my mother, Jean Gregory*, 2003, GW

↑ Cat.42 *Self-portrait as my father, Brian Wearing*, 2003, GW

← Cat.43 *Self-portrait as my grandmother, Nancy Gregory*, 2006, GW

↑ Cat.44 *Self-portrait as my grandfather, George Gregory*, 2006, GW

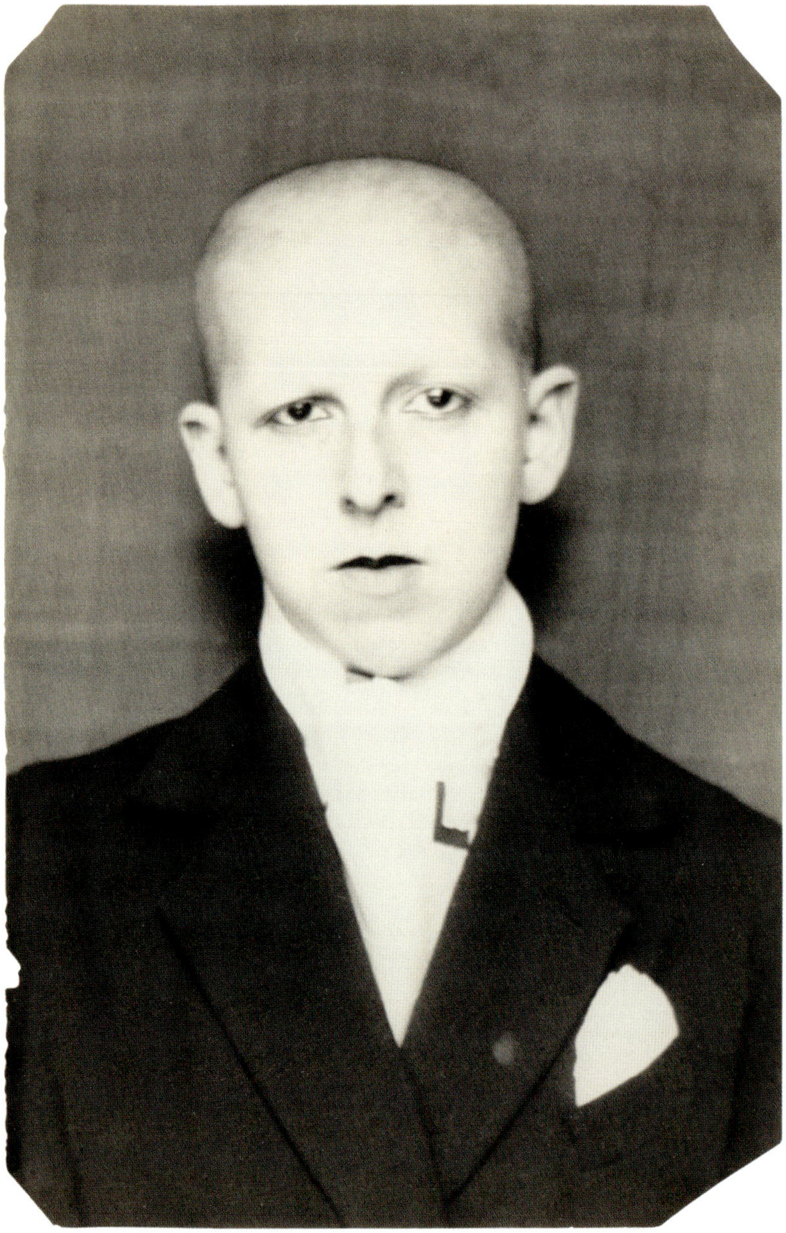

← Cat.45 *Self-portrait (as a dandy, head and shoulders)*, 1921–2, CC

↑ Cat.46 *Self-portrait (seated cross-legged like Buddha)*, 1927, CC

↑ Cat.47 *Self-portrait as my sister, Jane Wearing*, 2003, GW

→ Cat.48 *Self-portrait as my brother, Richard Wearing*, 2003, GW

← Cat.49 *Self-portrait (in cupboard)*, c.1932, CC

↑ Cat.50 *Self-portrait at three years old*, 2004, GW

MAMIYAFLEX

← Cat.51 *Me as Arbus*, 2008, GW

↑ Cat.52 *Me as Warhol in drag with scar*, 2010, GW

V

Masquerade

Gillian Wearing and Claude Cahun

Fig.13 *Marcel Duchamp as his* alter ego *Rrose Sélavy* by Man Ray, 1921

When Cahun was invited to write her autobiography she refused to make it autobiographical and instead wrote *Aveux non avenus*. In the same spirit we cannot assume that her self-portraits are direct reflections of herself. Since they were not intended for exhibition, Cahun rarely gave titles to her works at the time they were created. 'Self-portrait' was probably added to the title, together with a description of the work, by cataloguers and archivists, retrospectively. Wearing, who has always intended her work for exhibition, makes a playful and unexpected use of the word self-portrait in titles such as *Self-portrait of me now in mask*, (2011, cat.54). Playing on the temporal quality of photography and the fleetingness of the moment, as soon as the portrait was completed, it became a historical record of the artist in 2011 rather than a true contemporary depiction.

In the early part of the twentieth century the Surrealists were fascinated by Sigmund Freud's concept of the *alter ego*. Masquerade and the use of masks, both real and metaphorical, were adopted by artists of the time, including Marcel Duchamp, who famously dressed as Rrose Sélavy, his female *alter ego* (fig.13). Sélavy, whom Duchamp credited with some of his own artworks, went on to influence many younger artists who were critiquing strict gender distinctions, including Andy Warhol. Living in Paris as a student of philosophy and literature in the 1920s, Cahun would no doubt have been aware of Freud's concept of the *alter ego*. It is almost certain, too, that she would have encountered Duchamp's Rrose Sélavy.

Self-portrait (full-length masked figure in cloak with masks) (c.1928, cat.53) is an intriguing visualisation of Cahun's belief that she was made up of multiple selves. Cahun's use of masks, not only over her face but also stitched all over her cloak, suggests that she is attending a Venetian carnival with the decorative lace-curtain backdrop adding to the Italian flavour. It is possible that Moore, with her costume-design skills, was involved with the fabrication of this cape and attaching the masks. This self-portrait represents the many personalities of Cahun, and nowhere could her observation about the mask – 'Under this mask, another mask. I will never finish removing all these faces'[1] – be more appropriate. There is a marked difference between Cahun's use of the mask and Wearing's – whether Wearing is wearing the mask of her father, mother or three-year-old self, she still looks through the mask with her own eyes, whereas the eyes are filled in in Cahun's masks. Wearing has expressed her fascination with this work, and parallels can be drawn with Wearing's own use of masks. The artist has commented on this piece:

> The masks are both scary and beautiful at the same time ... I think this is one of the only surviving examples of Cahun actually wearing a mask. A lot of artists were interested in masks at the time – the Surrealists, Picasso ... but I've never seen an image like this from that era. In her photographs she's always discovering things outside the prevailing fashion.

Much of Cahun's work has been lost or destroyed, but it seems likely that she would have taken several variants of this image since she went to such great lengths to stage the photograph. Another self-portrait from the same series shows a masked Cahun sitting slumped in a chair and, again, the mask is without holes for the eyes (fig.15). The cropping of this portrait seems particularly contemporary in its treatment.

Cahun's *Self-portrait (in headscarf with mask in background)* (c.1929, cat.55) is one of the rare extant examples of Cahun including an actual full-face mask in her portraits and perhaps the image that comes closest to the way Wearing uses masks in her own self-portraits. In this *mise-en-scène* the painted mask, which again looks Venetian in style, is suspended from the screen backdrop, with Cahun in the foreground of the picture plane looking sidelong at the camera. In this work the artist reverts to the feminine, odalisque identity of her earlier portraits, which contrasts with the more stripped-back self-portraits created c.1920 (cats 15 and 18–19). Her own painted face echoes the stylised treatment of the mask, and she wears a long scarf wrapped around her head, a necklace and arm bracelet.

Cahun's self-portrait makes an interesting juxtaposition with Wearing's *Self-portrait of me now in mask* (2011, cat.54). Wearing a mask that is a replica of her face beneath, this can be seen as a reinterpretation of Cahun's concept that beneath this mask lies another mask *ad infinitum*. The suggestion is that one never knows the person beneath the mask; that, indeed, everyone, to a degree, is wearing a mask. The head-and-shoulders three-quarter-turn she adopts is a traditional pose for historical portraits. From the subtle palette of Wearing's top to the Renaissance blue-sky background, the photograph has an affinity with classical portrait painting.

Self-portrait (2000, cat.59) represents Wearing's first experimentation with the prosthetic mask and this hard mask is closer to the ones used by Cahun, in the unforgiving nature of the material. When Wearing began using masks, the fabrication methods were less sophisticated, and so it is, in a sense, more masklike and less like a second skin. The holes around the eyes and nostrils are quite crudely cut out compared with more recent images (fig.14). The artist's full-frontal pose, the symmetry and the striking use of colour – the green sweater and long black hair with straight fringe – make the portrait all the more arresting. The scale of this image is compelling too: it almost has the proportions of a billboard poster.

Self-portrait (kneeling, naked with mask) (c.1928, cat.56), is unusual in that Cahun created a studio setting outdoors. The *mise-en-scène* is altogether makeshift, domestic and otherworldly. The photograph was taken in bright sunlight, creating a harsh shadow along the top of the backdrop, which appears to be an eiderdown. Cahun presents herself like an Aztec worshipper, basking in the sunshine. Her skin is bronzed,

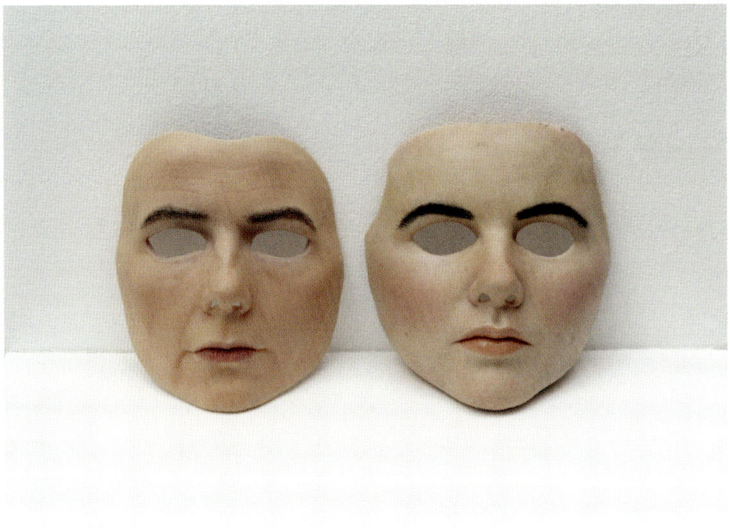

Fig.14 Masks used in *Me as Cahun holding a mask of my face* (left, cat.6) and *Self-portrait at twenty-seven years old* (right, cat.40) by Wearing

either by the sun or make-up. Her pose is symmetrical, with her hands resting on her shoulders and her feet folded behind her. Her mask is simple and doesn't cover her entire face.

As a teenager and then as a student, before she became aware that photography could be considered an art form, Wearing made sculptural pieces, influenced by Surrealism, as can be seen in her work *Me as an artist in 1984* (2014, cat.23). In 2013 she returned to making sculpture with her wax piece, *Me as mask* (cat.58). An intriguing and eerie assemblage, there are echoes of Cahun's eyeball piece (fig.11). The artist's hand holds the mask. Perhaps most disturbing of all, there are no eyes behind the mask, and that is what would make it human. It is as though the person behind the mask has been stripped away, leaving only the shell of the face.

In May 1936, Cahun exhibited in the *Exposition surréaliste d'objets* at Galerie Charles Ratton in Paris. Eskimo and Oceanic masks from the private collections of Surrealists, including André Breton, were included in the exhibition. In the summer of that year, Cahun visited the International Surrealist exhibition in Burlington Gardens, London. *Têtes de cristal (Crystal heads), British Museum, London* (June–July 1936, cat.57) records Cahun's visit to the Mexican and Aztec masks at the British Museum during that same trip. The artist's ghostly face appears, fleetingly, in the photograph, seen peering between the masks and above a caption card through the glass vitrine. Positioned on the same horizontal plane as the masks, Cahun's masklike face, framed with wisps of blonde hair, metamorphoses into another deathly head in the museum.

In *Self-portrait (in goggles)* (1927, cat.60), Cahun appears in heroic mode. While her lipstick and patterned neckscarf are feminine, her slicked-back hair is more masculine. It is possible that she is acting out the role of a female heroine of the time – Amy Johnson, the first woman to fly single-handedly from England to Australia. The goggles, her mask in this case, are blacked-out, making them difficult to interpret, and, of course, impossible to see through. Cahun's collection of stories, *Héroïnes*, subverts feminine stereotypes as portrayed through such legendary biblical and mythological heroines as Delilah and Judith, appropriating and reinterpreting them as possible images of herself. This could be one such example of Cahun reappropriating an image – creating a gender-neutral portrait of a contemporary heroine.

Sarah Howgate

1 Claude Cahun, *Disavowals or Cancelled Confessions*, trans. Susan de Muth (Tate, London, 2007), p.183.

← Cat.53 *Self-portrait (full-length masked figure in cloak with masks)*, c.1928, CC

↑ Fig.15 *Self-portrait (masked, slumped in chair)*, c.1928, CC

← Cat.54 *Self-portrait of me now in mask*, 2011, GW

↑ Cat.55 *Self-portrait (in headscarf with mask in background)*, c.1929, CC

Cat.56 *Self-portrait (kneeling, naked with mask)*, c.1928, CC

← Cat.57 *Têtes de cristal (Crystal heads), British Museum, London,* June–July 1936, CC

↑ Cat.58 *Me as mask*, 2013, GW

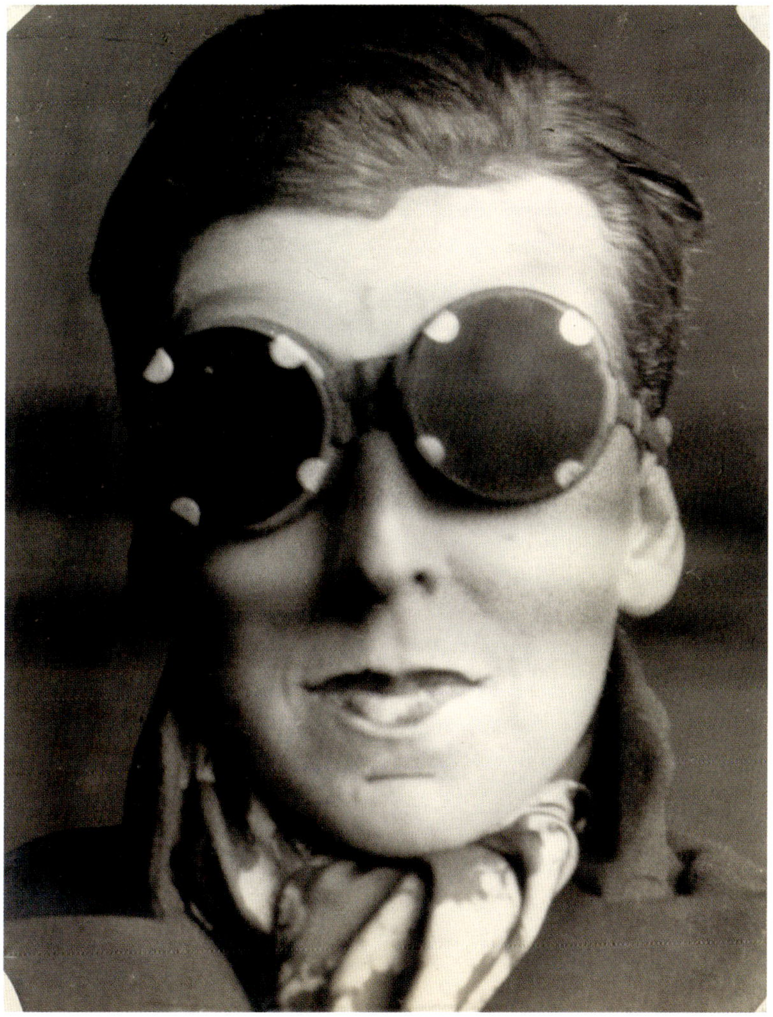

← Cat.59 *Self-portrait*, 2000, GW

↑ Cat.60 *Self-portrait (in goggles)*, 1927, CC

VI

Performance

Gillian Wearing and Claude Cahun

Fig.16 *Portrait bronze of Cahun* by Chana Orloff, 1921

In the video *Dancing in Peckham* (1994, cat.61), performance and self-presentation are combined to create a work that is not only a self-portrait but a portrait of someone else, apparently lost in their own private world. Wearing's inspiration for this piece was an anonymous woman she saw dancing with abandon at a jazz concert at the Royal Festival Hall on London's South Bank. In the 25-minute video Wearing re-enacts this observed performance, which she has taken out of context by transposing it from a central London cultural centre to the ordinariness of a South London shopping centre. While the soundtrack is the background noise of a busy shopping centre, echoing against the harsh surfaces, the music is only in her head and inaudible to passers-by (she cites artists including Gloria Gaynor and Michael Jackson and the band Nirvana as her musical inspiration). In a still taken from the video a boy wearing sunglasses walks behind Wearing, captivated by her performance, although she remains unaware. The image walks a tightrope between comic and tragic. Out of context the artist's behaviour appears deranged and uncomfortable to look at for passers-by, as they witness a private moment in a public space. Today people are highly conscious of how to present themselves through the medium of 'selfies', social media and even their own avatar world, but this seminal work was very much ahead of its time.

The documentary genre and method acting have influenced Wearing's performative work. By contrast, Cahun's own such work was influenced by the experimental and esoteric theatre of 1920s Paris. When Cahun moved to the city with Moore in the 1920s they became immersed in its cultural life, and the theatre became Cahun's great passion. Unlike the work she produced before and after this period, the self-portraits created in Paris present an outward act for the camera and an audience, rather than a more internalised, domestic performance. They represent a different aspect of self-portraiture, depicting the artist in role-play, being someone else, in a similar way to Wearing. It is known that Moore was integral to Cahun's performance works – she both created the costumes and took the photographs. *Self-portrait* (1929, cat.64) is a close-up head-and-shoulders portrait of Cahun as Satan in the theatre piece *Le Mystère d'Adam,* an adaptation of a twelfth-century mystery play about Adam and Eve. Most probably taken by Moore, this is one of a series in which Cahun reworks the image several times. In this stark and symmetrical portrait Cahun's direct gaze is engaging and formidable, while her gender remains uncertain. Cahun's painted-on double eyebrows and burnished skin resonate with the modernist sculpture of the time and in particular Russian artist Chana Orloff's portrait bronze of Cahun of 1921 (fig.16).

Cahun's capacity for transformation and the performative led her to take on several different roles, including that of Bluebeard's wife. Set against a theatrical backdrop in *Self-portrait (as Elle in* Barbe-Bleue*)* (1929, cat.65), Cahun adopts an exaggerated female role with a painted, doll-like face and plaits wound around the crown of her head. In a cropped variant of this image (fig.18), Cahun's angled, head-and-shoulders pose is mirrored and superimposed on another version of the same character. The doubling of the image illustrates the artist's experimental approach and echoes the collaged works in *Aveux non avenus*, in which heads appear totem-like on top of other heads (see cat.29). Wearing comments on this portrait:

> *There are a lot of similarities between this and* Que me veux-tu? *[1928, fig.10]. Although the facial expressions are quite similar, there is less tension between the two Claudes in this image. This is different from her other self-portraits. You can almost see in her eyes that she is performing for someone else rather than herself or Marcel.*

In contrast to this image of femininity, in *Self-portrait (as Monsieur in* Banlieu*)* (1929, cat.63), Cahun presents herself, unequivocally, as a man, with her suit and tie, and cropped hair, dyed black. In this guise she is barely recognisable as Cahun, the drawn eyebrows being the only give-away. The blurred portrait has the quality of a snapshot – she is caught in role in the moment.

Self-portrait (with globe) (c.1927, fig.19) demonstrates a different kind of performance with Cahun acting out one of her many selves rather than a theatrical hero. Her face is the colour of white porcelain and contrasts dramatically with her painted dark, scalloped hairline. Cahun's bronzed arms in symmetrical formation prefigure the artist's use of isolated limbs in the collages for *Aveux non avenus*. The globe reflects the photographer, most likely to be Moore, and the reflections also reference Narcissus. Wearing comments:

> *She looks very masculine, even though she's wearing a lot of make-up. She reminds me of singer-songwriter Marc Almond. And the globe's hard to read, but I can see the room, and the window reflected in it. The globe could be seen as an all-seeing eye. Cahun was drawn to eyes in her collages. I wonder if this was intended for use in a collage, since all the details seem to be in her face, arms and globe, and the rest of the composition is less carefully considered. For example, the shawl seems out of place. Maybe it was meant to be cropped.*

In 1928 Cahun created a series of semaphore-like images. In *Self-portrait (aerial view on blanket)*, she used her body to create letters of the alphabet including 'M' for Marcel (cat.66) and 'C' for Claude (cat.67). Photographed outdoors in harsh sunlight, the shadow of the wrought-iron balcony is visible on one side of the white cloth.

There are several variants of *Self-portrait (reflected image in mirror with chequered jacket)* (1927, cat.68), but this crop, in which Cahun grips the neck of her jacket and the background details of the room are removed, is the most arresting. Moore, too, took up this pose, perhaps as a preparatory set-up, but the contrast between the two images highlights the strengths of Cahun's self-portrait work. In Cahun's own portrait she has golden hair and bronzed skin in contrast to Moore's more conventional appearance and relaxed pose (fig.17). Playing on the notion of Narcissus and duality, Cahun is not actually looking into the mirror, but the mirror, with its reflection, provides two versions of the artist – one looking intently at the viewer and the other looking away. Wearing comments:

> *It's the idea of the double, the doubling-up, twin and mirror image, with the persona and the split personality.*
>
> *Marcel's version of the self-portrait is more like a snapshot, and her expression looks as if she is slightly embarrassed by the act of posing, whereas Claude's pose is confident and direct. And that's interesting because, if you think about Surrealist photography, there were a lot of male photographers taking photographs of women as objects, parts of machinery, such as Man Ray's [1933] image of Meret Oppenheim naked beside the flywheel of a printing press. And Claude was working at the same time, a woman who was totally in control of her own image.*

In *Self-portrait (in national dress)* (c.1938, cat.70), Cahun is seen in a striking three-quarter-length pose, again looking directly out at the viewer with a similar expression to that in her *Self-portrait (reflected image in mirror with chequered jacket)* of 1927. Wearing a non-specific 'national costume', an exotic, patterned design with an ornamented headdress and long Viking-queen plaits, Cahun is adopting another persona, although it is uncertain who this character might be. Moore's own background in fashion illustration would perhaps have influenced the pose as well as the costume (fig.25).

Self-portrait (on sea wall at La Rocquaise) (1947, cat.62) is a series of contact sheets that record Cahun, after her release from prison and the Liberation of Jersey, at the bottom of her garden dancing on a sea wall erected by the Germans during the Occupation. With each pose subtly different, they appear like stills from a movie. Although she is now in her fifties, there is a youthfulness and freedom about the manner of her poses and diaphanous clothing. In one image (page 119), she looks like Bo Peep holding her crook. In another (page 121, bottom right), she has the appearance of a young bride wearing a veil. After the terrible deprivation and confines of prison life, she presents herself as a free spirit with the beautiful backdrop of St Brelade's Bay behind her.

Sarah Howgate

Fig.17 *Marcel Moore (reflected in mirror)*, 1928, CC

← Cat.61a *Dancing in Peckham*, still from video, 1994, GW

↑ Cat.62a *Self-portrait (on sea wall at La Rocquaise)*, 1947, CC

← Cat.61b *Dancing in Peckham*, stills from video, 1994, GW

↑ Cat.62b Contact sheets from *Self-portrait (on sea wall at La Rocquaise)*, 1947, CC

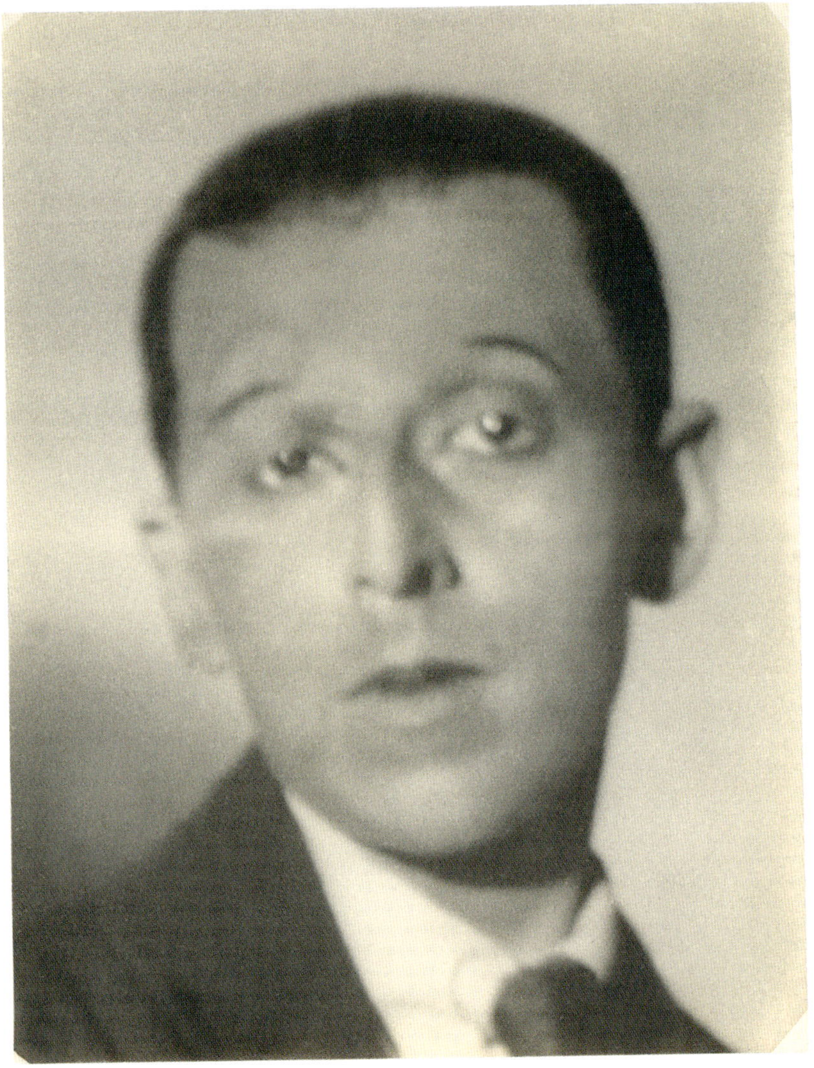

← Cat.63 *Self-portrait (as Monsieur in* Banlieu*)*, 1929, CC

↑ Cat.64 *Self-portrait (as le Diable in* Le Mystère d'Adam*)*, 1929, CC

↑ Fig.18 *Self-portrait (double head image as Elle in* Barbe-Bleue*)*, 1929, CC

→ Cat.65 *Self-portrait (as Elle in* Barbe-Bleue*)*, 1929, CC

← Cats 66 and 67 *Self-portrait (aerial view on blanket)*, 1928, CC

↑ Fig.19 *Self-portrait (with globe)*, c.1927, CC

← Cat.68 *Self-portrait (reflected image in mirror with chequered jacket)*, 1927, CC

↑ Cat.69 *Mirror*, 2016, GW

Cat.70 *Self-portrait (in national dress)*, c.1938, CC

VII

Later life and memento mori

Gillian Wearing and Claude Cahun

In contrast to her earlier work, the self-portraits Cahun made in later life are generally more feminine and less androgynous. In the late 1930s, before the outbreak of war, she and Moore created a series of intriguing performative self-portraits. 'Les mesdames', as she and Moore were known by the locals, continued practising their bohemian lifestyle. Naked sunbathing and a love of dressing up and performance didn't fade. In *Self-portrait (naked with leaves)* (1938, cat.71), Cahun appears dressed in fig leaves against a backdrop of foliage. In *Self-portrait (with leopard skin)* (1939, cat.72), Cahun looks like an actor playing an historical character in a Hollywood silent movie, perhaps one of her heroines, Delilah or Cleopatra. She wears a dark wig with ringlets and rests on one elbow. There is a hint of exoticism, certainly eroticism, as she reclines among the lush bedding plants, clutching a bunch of grapes. In the lying-down variant (cat.73) there is the suggestion that she has been laid to rest. Bizarrely her cat is dressed in leopard-skin clothing, too. In *Self-portrait (in velvet dress in front of La Rocquaise arch)* (1939, cat.75), she stands eyes shut in an elegant, full-length velvet dress with hand on hip, like a fashion-plate model or châtelaine at the entrance to her home. In *Self-portrait (in barn doorway)* (1938, cat.74), another full-length standing pose, she wears a long silk dress and hairnet. Hand on hip, she is framed by the barn doorway, the interior creating a dark backdrop. *Self-portrait (in cloak with cloaked figure)* (1939, cat.76), is perhaps a nod to her Surrealist past – eyes closed again wearing a long black cloak she is accompanied by an objectified version of herself. The mannequin 'twin' is dressed in a similar cloak and has a mop of hair, perhaps created from dried hydrangeas. There are more performative images from this period, too. *Self-portrait (with round frame)* (c.1938, cat.77) shows Cahun, dressed in a housecoat, holding a circular frame around her face, turning herself into a conventional oil painting. *Self-portrait (standing and sitting in garden)* (1939, cat.79), is a double-exposure image that shows the landscape 'reflected', like a Rorschach test. The view of the bay is seen through the aperture of an eye – a recurring motif for Cahun. From a series of photographs of Cahun sitting on a ledge behind latticed windows, *Self-portrait (in window of La Rocquaise)* (c.1938, cat.78), shows Cahun imprisoned in her home, a grim portent of what was to come.

Of course throughout her years in prison the artist did not produce any images – only letters remain. On release from prison the couple found their home had been ransacked, and many of Cahun's photographs destroyed. Despite the hardships they had suffered, in *Self-portrait (with Nazi badge between teeth)* (1945, cat.80) Cahun remains strikingly defiant. Dressed more conventionally – the decorative headscarf has replaced the bleached, cropped hair – Cahun remains playful. She holds a Nazi badge, given to her by the prison guards, whom she befriended, between her teeth. The image reveals remarkable courage and bravery. Wearing comments:

She was an activist as well as an artist, who didn't think in straightforward ways. The whole prison experience sounded like it was very complex, one failed suicide attempt, two from Moore. The women were prepared to face their execution and wouldn't sign an appeal against it because they believed in continued resistance. Yet they also managed to befriend some of the guards. Cahun's behaviour never followed a conventional path. The idea that there was some level of discussion to be had was intelligent and brave. She turned the prison guards' minds around because obviously she believed in the power of good as well as indirect action. That's why she gave out propaganda leaflets. She could be quite selfless. On an island there's no real escape, and neither did they try to. She and Moore were always prepared to die for the cause.

Made two years later, *Self-portrait (with masked face and graveyard)* (c.1947, cat.81), is one of a series of photographs taken in the garden with the churchyard in the distance. These images, with Cahun posing like an angel statue from a Victorian cemetery, have a remarkable poignancy, given that the artist was to be buried there only seven years later. (For Wearing's response to the work, see cat.7.) Wearing comments:

She's wearing a mask, which almost looks like a bowl. There's a suggestion, because of the setting and the fact that she looks like an angel, that she's thinking about death. I wonder how ill she was at this point, as she had had heart disease for many years.

Around the same time, Cahun made another series in which she appears to confront death with defiance. In *Self-portrait (with cat, skull and gravestones)* (c.1947, cat.84), she adopts a masculine pose, smoking a cigarette against a backdrop of tombstones. At her feet is her cat; in the foreground is the skull of a small animal. Ten years earlier, the skull appears in *Self-portrait (in doorway of La Rocquaise)* (1937, cat.83), a full-length portrait in which she holds the skull in her hand. *Le chemin des chats V (Cats' lane V)* (c.1948, cat.82) shows her wearing a blindfold and eccentrically walking her cat on a lead.

The final image of Cahun and Moore taken in 1950 (cat.86) shows them in bathing suits of contrasting colours, posing either side of an archway in the garden at La Rocquaise. Hauntingly, Cahun's face and torso have been defaced, although by whom remains a mystery.

Although she has only reached middle age, Wearing shares Cahun's concerns with the transience of life and the passage of time. *Me as a clock* (1990, cat.87), is literally a time-based media work and an example of movement that has been stilled. Wearing had her photograph taken and printed onto a clock at the children's toy store, Hamleys, in London. Wearing recounts how she insisted on moving around during the sitting, much to the irritation of the shop photographer. Her face, captured in motion, was then superimposed on the clock. Preserved by Wearing in its original cardboard box, this clock piece is a symbol of time passing. Wearing was still young, and the clock's hands record the passage of time as they move over her face, on the clock's own face. Behind Wearing's image are the ghosts of other figures – she is merely a face in the crowd.

Wearing's *Me as a ghost* (2015, cat.90) relates to Cahun's late work. Her T-shirt, emblazoned with the words 'Heavy Metal', refers to Wearing's own heritage – the metal groups that formed in the West Midlands in the late 1960s when the artist was growing up, and Birmingham's place at the heart of the Industrial Revolution. Wearing could be at a rock concert, surrounded by fake smoke; or she could literally be going up in smoke. Wearing's *Me as Mapplethorpe* (2009, cat.91), part of her 'Spiritual Family' series, replicates Mapplethorpe's original photograph, unlike the others in the series (page 82). Mapplethorpe, with Wearing behind the mask, is staring death in the face. With a skull on top of his staff, he represents the grim reaper. Wearing remarks: 'I had to ensure my eyes held the same psychological expression as his: a look of inner turbulence but very much alive.'

In *Rock 'n' roll 70* (2015, cat.88), Wearing produced a diptych that, if she lives to the age of seventy, will become a triptych. On the left is a rare photograph of Wearing, unmasked, as she was in 2015. In the centre is a computer-generated impression of how she might look at seventy: the signature long hair remains, although it is tinged with grey; she has become stooped. To the right is an empty space reserved for a photograph of Wearing if she does live to the age of seventy. The wallpaper portraits *Rock 'n' roll 70 wallpaper* (2015–16, cat.92) are a similar construct. Sometimes working with forensic artists, but more recently undertaking the technical work herself, Wearing has produced her own impressions of how she might age – some images show the effects of facial surgery, breast enhancement, changing hairstyles and dress. In one image, referencing the 'Family Album' series, Wearing acts out a saccharine studio portrait in which she poses as two versions of herself in different roles – as her older self putting her arms around her younger, present-day self. Another shows a double portrait of Wearing with her partner Michael Landy imagined at seventy.

In 2016, Wearing produced her own version of the Exquisite Corpse: a chance-based parlour game played by the Surrealists in which each participant draws on a sheet of paper, folds it to conceal their drawing and then passes it to the next player for their contribution. Wearing collaborated with Landy and her friend Gary Hume on a composite portrait of herself, titled *My exquisite corpse* (2016, cat.94). The contributions of Hume (the head) and Landy (the torso) were hidden when Wearing produced the legs and feet. In a further nod to Surrealism, Wearing drew four legs, like those of the stool on which she sits.

In 2012, Wearing made *Me as my ideal self* (cat.89), a painting of an ever-youthful Wearing, airbrushed and breast-enhanced, standing on a crate in supermodel pose. This work opens out like a book: inside is a family-album reconstruction in the form of a Victorian screen, collaged with multiple self-portraits.

Earlier in her career, before she began the 'Family Album' series, Wearing made a two-minute video of her grandmother, *Nancy Gregory* (2002, cat.93), based on a snapshot that her mother took. With the brightly coloured hydrangeas nodding in the late-summer sun and the flies buzzing around the static image of the old lady, this is a *memento mori* in the classical sense. Wearing has put herself in her grandmother's skin. It offers a different interpretation of old age to her more defiant *Rock 'n' roll 70* (cat.88), or Cahun's *Self-portrait (on sea wall at La Rocquaise)* (cat.62). There is nothing enhanced about this image.

Sarah Howgate

Cat.71 *Self-portrait (naked with leaves)*, 1938, CC

← Cat.72 *Self-portrait (with leopard skin)*, 1939, CC

↑ Cat.73 *Self-portrait (lying on leopard skin)*, 1939, CC

← Cat.74 *Self-portrait (in barn doorway)*, 1938, CC

↑ Cat.75 *Self-portrait (in velvet dress in front of La Rocquaise arch)*, 1939, CC

← Cat.76 *Self-portrait (in cloak with cloaked figure)*, 1939, CC

↑ Cat.77 *Self-portrait (with round frame)*, c.1938, CC

← Cat.78 *Self-portrait (in window of La Rocquaise)*, c.1938, CC

↑ Cat.79 *Self-portrait (standing and sitting in garden)*, 1939, CC

← Cat.80 *Self-portrait (with Nazi badge between teeth)*, 1945, CC

↑ Cat.81 *Self-portrait (with masked face and graveyard)*, c.1947, CC

← Cat.82 *Le chemin des chats V (Cats' lane V)*, c.1948, CC

↖ Cat.83 *Self-portrait (in doorway of La Rocquaise)*, 1937, CC

↑ Cat.84 *Self-portrait (with cat, skull and gravestones)*, c.1947, CC

↗ Cat.85 *Self-portrait (with skull and cigarette)*, 1947, CC

← Cat.86 *Marcel Moore and Claude Cahun*, 1950, CC

↑ Cat.87 *Me as a clock*, 1990, GW

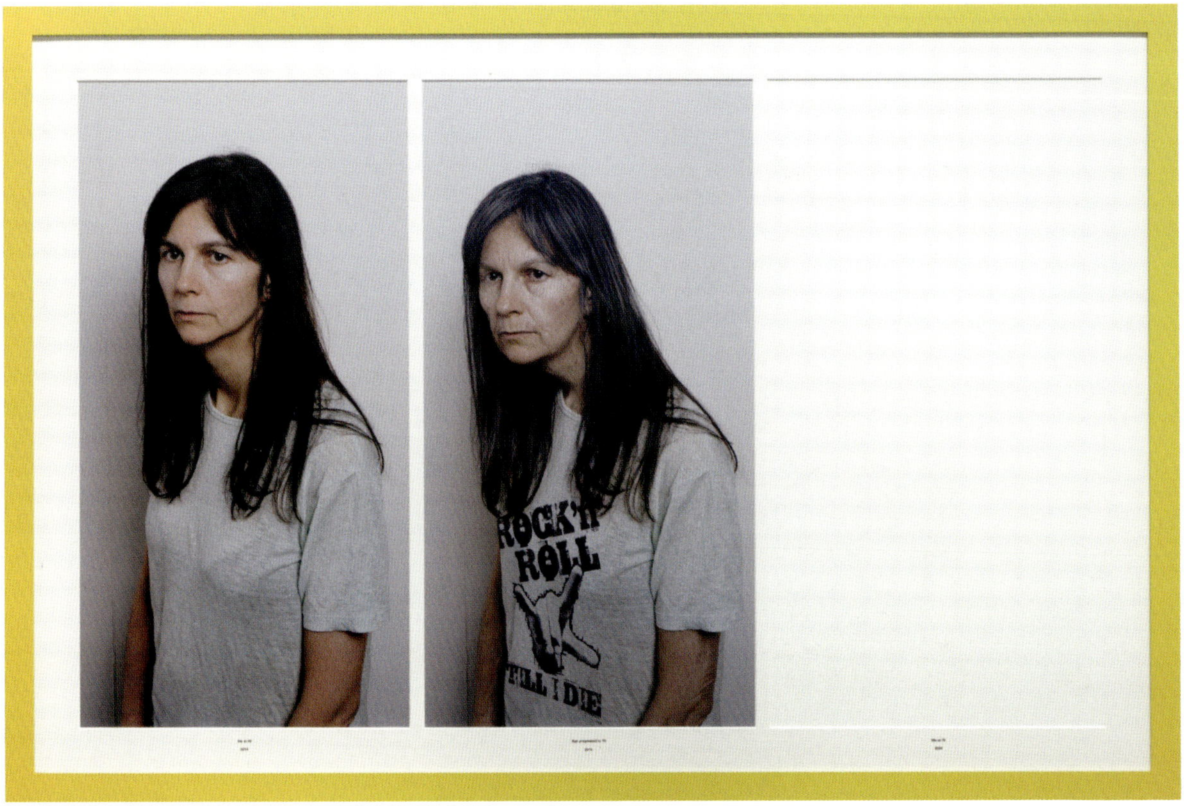

↑ Cat.88 *Rock 'n' roll 70*, 2015, GW

→ Cat.89 *Me as my ideal self*, 2012, GW

COR!
WHAT A BARGAIN
1859

HEAVY
METAL

← Cat.90 *Me as a ghost*, 2015, GW

↑ Cat.91 *Me as Mapplethorpe*, 2009, GW

↓ Cat.92 *Rock 'n' roll 70 wallpaper*, 2015–16, GW

↑ Cat.93 *Nancy Gregory*, still from video, 2002, GW

→ Cat.94 *My exquisite corpse*, 2016, GW (Gary Hume (head), Michael Landy (torso) and Gillian Wearing (legs))

TO EXPERINCE
SOMETHING YOU
HAVE TO EXIST

Gillian Wearing in conversation with Sarah Howgate

London, 28 January and 11 February 2016

Fig.20 Wearing in St Brelade's Bay, Jersey.
Photo by Sarah Howgate, 2016

The 'Family Album'

SH I thought your 'Family Album' series would be a good place to start, and I wanted to ask about your first portrait in the series, *Self-portrait as my mother, Jean Gregory* [2003, cat.41]?

GW I had this image of my mother as a young woman for many years, although I didn't realise she was young until I looked at the photograph again in 2002. Up until that point I had this idea of it being of a much older woman. I had kept that age disparity between me and her in my mind and had aged the photograph along with that, and so it was a revelation to see that she was twenty-two, and I was thirty-nine. I have this memory of me holding the photograph in the living room of my flat; then having the idea of becoming her and re-creating the photograph [fig.21]. I also, at that point, realised she wasn't my mother when the studio shot was taken and hadn't even met my father, but I had for many years attached that role to her in the image, not thinking about her life outside of that. In the picture she looks like a young, optimistic woman – there is this potential and hope – and this look never happens again in the later images.

SH I'm interested in how you see the photograph that you created as the original, rather than the studio photograph on which it's based.

Fig.21 Wearing posing as her mother without a mask during the staging of *Self-portrait as my mother, Jean Gregory*, 2003

GW I'm aware of how the original source image looks. But I feel I have magnified my feelings of what I saw in that and transformed it from something conventional. The decisions I make in what I see and draw out in the images are personal, but the fact that I inhabit my mother is revelatory and reflects something larger than my own biography; it allows other people to think of their own relations. It reminds me of that Diane Arbus quote 'the more specific you are, the more general it'll be'. That's also why I chose to be my whole immediate family and re-create this idea of an album. I wanted to portray them all at a similar age, dispelling the hierarchy of who was born first or where the power lines lay, and highlighting the differences and similarities we all had as young people. Although of course all the eyes are mine, I am the one returning the gaze. So in the series, there is me as my mother, father, sister, brother, uncle and myself at seventeen. Then my grandfather and grandmother, portrayed at an older age.

SH Could you tell me more about the process of creating the 'Family Album'?

GW It took a long time to find a process that would work for the masks. I didn't want prosthetics. I always wanted it to be a mask that would completely cover my face and sometimes neck or, in my brother's case, upper body. I wanted them not only to look as real as possible but also to have certain parts of the disguise visible. Like the cut-outs around the eyes. Not immediately noticeable on a lot of images unless you look close. The mask has an imprint of my face inside. There are two faces on the mask, so even before I wear it as my own face I am already in there. And, unlike Photoshopping and retouching, wearing someone's face or body brings out a much stronger performative element in me. That's the thing, with all of these works, it's not just about wearing a mask but about becoming someone else, too, acting out. It's liberating to feel like another person and take on the traits you have observed or think they have. The whole thing becomes psychologically charged. A lot of the acting happens in the eyes or posture; so when I edit the images the eyes are one of the first things I choose. If you take your concentration away for one second it shows, and if you overact that also doesn't work. The process of making each mask up to the photographic stage takes about three to four months, during which hair for the eyebrows and head are punched into the mask; it's painted, I sometimes have sets built for the image, although the one of my brother was photographed in the original location.

SH Why did you choose that particular photograph of your brother as the starting point for *Self-portrait as my brother, Richard Wearing* [2003, cat.48]?

GW I loved this image as soon as I saw it in 1990. It sits like an anomaly among the more standard images my mother took; it goes beyond the cliché of a family snapshot, showing my brother in a private moment. It is like a modern version of a *vanitas*. He is caught off guard and not posing. At the time I thought it would make an interesting artwork but didn't know what to do with it until thirteen years later.

SH Another intriguing thing about this self-portrait as your brother is that, at the time, you recognised it as a contemporary image, in the sense that it was unstaged. But in re-creating the image you were making something that was completely staged, creating this tableau, if you like, of a young man at his *toilette*. I see a relationship here with the way Claude Cahun worked, in that nothing was left to chance in her self-portraits.

GW Yes, it was the most difficult of all shoots. The body mask was silicone and 3 inches [8cm] thick in parts. It left me with visible lumps on my shoulders for weeks. I had a gap at the back so my skin could breathe, but I am also wearing a bodystocking; so I was very hot underneath. The mouth was sealed shut, and I could only shallow-breathe through my nostrils. I didn't think I was going to survive five minutes but managed four hours. Many people did not believe there was a woman underneath that body. Someone wrote that I had digitally put my eyes into an old snapshot but didn't question the high image quality (taken on a medium-format camera) or that a 5-foot-high [1.5-metre] snapshot might be grainy and soft. So, the disbelief was a kind of backhanded compliment based on how convincing it looks.

Me as an artist

SH I want to move on to your development as an artist, focusing on your work, *Me as an artist in 1984* [2014, cat.23].

GW This represents a time before I thought of myself as an artist. I left school at sixteen without qualifications and for six years worked in various office jobs. In my spare time I made drawings, small sculptures and even paintings. The image I recreated is of me sitting on a chest of drawers, surrounded by a few pieces of artwork I had made. In retrospect you can see how this led to me becoming an artist, but I didn't know that was going to be my future at that time. It was a year later, in 1985, that I left my job as a secretary to go to art school. We can all choose images from our life that shape our narratives and give us a plausible sense of our identity, and this is a defining one for me. My inspirations at the time were Surrealism and Dalí; I was also into masks, having made some at senior school and the art teacher raving about them. You can see a papier-mâché mask I remade in this image. There is a small sculpture of a person regurgitating themselves (their body is coming out of their mouths) – something I tried to articulate in drawings and sculpture, but it never really worked out. Here it is next to me on the chest of drawers. I made a lot of these figures using self-drying clay. I had been making figurines like this since I was around fourteen, so there was obviously an interest in art from an early age, even though I gave it up in the third year at secondary school.

I built a replica of the room in which I used to live in Earls Court, in my studio; I collaborated with an art director who had also worked on my feature film *Self Made* [2011]. We studied the original image and noticed how much damp there was on the walls, something about which I had been oblivious when I was younger and used to living in run-down properties. We copied that detail, and it looked quite over the top until I compared it with the original after the shoot and realised we had been quite conservative. We also hired and adapted furniture and props; found replica hair-spray cans, 1980s ornaments. I suppose it is a perverse idea to spend so much time re-creating an image that initially took a brief few moments to make.

SH You said in the catalogue for your Institut Valencià d'Art Modern (IVAM) exhibition that, while you can't remember what it was like to be in the body of a twenty-one year old, you do recall the experience of how it felt to be in that room with the mould on the walls.[1]

GW We become such different people over time, and it's hard to hold on to what we feel in any given moment. Moments pass. It's almost like you think you'll always know yourself, but from experiences in life we change a lot. When I put on that mask for *Me as an artist in 1984* [2014], I didn't have the same slight ignorance or naivety that I had in the original photograph. But even ten years from now, I'll probably think that I had certain naiveties when I took the photograph in 2014. When you look at something you can dissect it in time but not in that moment.

My Polaroid years

SH With the Polaroids that you took in the 1980s and 1990s, you must have really thought about each photograph?

GW It was always a thrill to use the camera and get an instant image. I experimented to get the best shots and used objects like a coat hanger or driftwood to take an image from a further distance. I joke that these are my prehistoric 'selfie sticks'.

SH You didn't date them systematically?

GW Some have months; a lot of them have years on them. I think I dated them when I was invited to do an artist's page in the *Observer* in 1998, with more than sixty Polaroids over two pages. I wanted to show their chronology; so they started in December 1988 and went up to 1998.

SH It seems that it is only when you are revisiting them now that objects are emerging in the background that you didn't realise were there at the time, such as, for example, the envy mask?

GW I wasn't thinking of the context in which I was photographing myself; I was just taking the photographs to see how I looked or if I could change or adapt my look. After a few years I realised these photographs had become a document; it was about all those incremental changes that happen in your face or attitude. The places where I lived, the rooms I inhabited and all the detritus around me. The fact that they are self-portraits meant they became a series by default. You only really notice the differences when you lay out the photographs side by side. It's interesting seeing them now in terms of 'selfies'. Some of my poses in the series are similar to how people pose for 'selfies' now. The difference is mine were strictly for my own consumption, not for friends or family. Also they were taken many years before social media. They fit into my larger body of work, like *10–16* [1997], where actors lip-synch to children's voices from the age of ten to sixteen. Or my recent work *Rock 'n' roll 70* [2015, cat.88], where I am age-progressed to seventy. This work consists of three window mounts in one frame, the first showing me at fifty, the second age-progressed to seventy, and the final mount is left blank. In the event of me reaching seventy I will add the actual photograph in 2034. If I don't reach that milestone then it will be for everyone else to imagine how I might have looked. The framed work has been exhibited, and hung on wallpaper featuring other versions of me at seventy. I wanted to go beyond the stereotype that older age homogenises everyone and show that your identity/lifestyle/work can still be in flux and changeable. It is not about who you once were but who you are at any age.

The 'Spiritual Family' series

SH Can we move on to the artists who have been important to you and those you have become in some of your self-portraits? Let's start with *Me as Warhol in drag with scar* [2010, cat.52]. What did you admire particularly about Warhol and what made you want to become him?

GW My first memorable experience of contemporary art was seeing Warhol at an exhibition on pop art in Birmingham. When I moved to London, in 1983, I saw an all-night screening of *Ciao! Manhattan*, starring Edie Sedgwick. Most films I'd seen up until then had a story, or some kind of linear plot, and here I was looking at some people improvising on a couch. I became fascinated with Warhol's background and bought books about him and Sedgwick and the Factory lifestyle [fig.22]. I'd been fashion conscious – punk, goth, New Romantic – when I was younger; like Warhol, I wanted to belong to a counter-culture. People associate Warhol with his screenprints, but I think his film work was more seminal and has influenced me more.

For instance, my film *Family History* [2006, fig.23] is based on *The Family*, a twelve-part TV documentary by Paul Watson that followed a working-class family from Reading in 1974. This had been influenced by *An American Family*, released in the US the year before, featuring the Louds, a quintessential American Dream family, middle-class and attractive, who allowed their lives and a marriage break-up to be filmed. It was a huge TV hit; the first example of fly-on-the-wall television and very Warholian, replicating the idea of filming people all day long and in lingering takes.

Fig.22 Andy Warhol filming *Chelsea Girls* in New York. Photograph by Santi Visalli, 4 May 1966

Fig.23 *Family History* catalogue cover by Wearing, 2007

Me as Warhol in drag with scar is from a series I call my 'Spiritual Family': artists who have been important to me and my greater guidance in life. All of them worked in photography and with issues of identity, masks, documentary. *Me as Mapplethorpe* [2009, cat.91] is based on the last self-portrait he took before he died from AIDS in 1989, and I think it is the strongest photographic self-portrait ever to have dealt with mortality; it's also a beautiful image. Mapplethorpe looks directly at the lens; only his face and hand are lit. His cheekbones, protruding from his gaunt face, echo that of the skull on top of the walking cane he is holding; his head appears disembodied and floating in space. This was from an artist whose recording of other people held no inhibitions; he didn't shy away from any theme, including his own illness. There is nothing in the image I wanted to change. I think we can all put ourselves in a position of someone who is dying; it's something, as a living person, I try at times to make sense of. When I looked at Mapplethorpe's original image I wanted to understand what he was feeling: is it physical or emotional pain, or both? The importance of photography is how it shapes reflections of ourselves. His mask is both a mask for me to be him and a death mask. It was important I was granted permission from the Robert Mapplethorpe Foundation for this. The mask that was made for the shoot is a meticulous rendition of this final period in his life. I had to ensure my eyes held the same psychological expression as his: a look of inner turbulence but very much alive. We all have masks and behind someone's mask is always a torrent of conflicting emotions and thoughts.

On Cahun and collaboration

SH In terms of your 'Spiritual Family', when did you first come across Claude Cahun's work, and what intrigued you about her?

GW I recall a series of her self-portrait images in a newspaper in the mid-1990s, in which it was claimed that she had just been 'discovered', although people had known about her photographs years earlier. Her work felt relevant, and twenty years later it still does. The fact that she created different guises in her images makes me realise that is something innate; we all role-play. When I was younger my friends and I would pose for photographs. The images were performative; we took our cues from fashion and music magazines [fig.24].

SH When you were what sort of age?

GW Probably around sixteen to seventeen. When I look at some of Cahun's images, I imagine that some of her poses mimicked commercial images of the times. Her partner, Marcel Moore, created fashion illustrations [fig.25]. Women's roles were changing in the 1920s, along with the fashion for flatter chests, shorter hair and wearing trousers. This could have been an inspiration.

SH There's also a question around Marcel Moore's role in Claude Cahun's creative production and what you as an artist think that might have been?

GW Marcel was an accomplished illustrator, but her work didn't have any of Claude's 'off the wall' qualities. So, by default, I feel Claude had the main say in her own work. Obviously, anyone in a close relationship can help through their understanding of another person's practice over many years. Marcel could have suggested props or poses. But to me it feels like the signature of one person, and that's Cahun. If you look at the photographs taken by Marcel when Claude's not in the work they are unremarkable. Also when Marcel's in the shot she's unable to project a different persona in the same way that Claude does [see fig.17]. So I would suggest Marcel was a creative enabler.

SH And that's different from your own relationship with Michael [Landy], because he's a successful artist in his own right.

GW What's good about us both being artists is that we're able to speak about our work. We know each other's practice in depth and have a lot of similar views about art, so that does help.

Fig.24 Wearing in hairdressing magazine *Hair and Beauty*, June 1987. Photo by Kriss Hass

Fig.25 Fashion illustration by Marcel Moore, 1915

SH There's a difference too in your own approach to artistic production. When you're making a film or a photograph, you commission technicians to create the prosthetics, and Cahun didn't have any of that kind of technical support.

GW Andy Warhol is credited for many works that were made under his name at the Factory. His team and collaborators knew his vision, and that seeped into everything to create the 'Warhol' look. In Claude's case, it wasn't a factory situation but one supportive partner.

SH It's also interesting to note that Cahun thought of herself as a writer rather than an artist.

GW Her work had a very improvised look. It's thrilling to see how many photographs she made; the fact she persevered with them and had a compulsion to make images throughout her life.

SH Yes, although inevitably the Second World War and her imprisonment had an impact on her work. After she was released from prison she produced less work, and by then, of course, she was older.

GW I wonder if we should consider her appearance as well. She had a face that was highly adaptable. As she got older we see her using transformation less. Perhaps this is something to do with the need to fit into Jersey society or the trauma of being imprisoned.

SH When you made *Me as Cahun holding a mask of my face* [2012, cat.6], how did you decide which elements of Cahun's original photograph to use and how did you make it your own?

GW I didn't want to repeat 'I am in training don't kiss me' but bring instead an aspect of myself. So I decided to hold a mask I made of my face that year; so we are seeing my face divorced from my eyes. There are three masks in the photograph: me underneath my mask, Cahun's mask and the mask of me. Cahun played along with these slippages, through adopting different guises; that's what I'm doing, too. Where am I in this? How can you know me or her? How can we ever know ourselves? What I've learnt from using the mask is that when you put it on, the eyes do so much to bring alive what is essentially a shell. And you can differentiate the female and male eye. Even with my dad's mask, which looks very masculine, my eyes don't look at all like a man's. Yet, from a certain distance, it is a convincing transformation.

On spiritual camaraderie

SH When it comes to the comparisons between your work and Cahun's, what are the challenges for you, as a contemporary artist, of exhibiting alongside Cahun? There's a difference in scale and in the surfaces of your images, for obvious reasons. Aesthetically, they're different too, but they share universal themes.

GW We both have been interested in constructions of identity, of taking images of being male, female and the transitions between the two. In fact in my '[Family] Album' and 'Spiritual Family' series I have been a man more than a woman, a point that has never been brought up. It also struck me that a lot of my work is about going back and entering moments in either my own life or another person's life. Claude, I feel, has played more with invented characters and personae.

I'm glad there are also differences in scale – artists did not print their work large in Cahun's era, and that needs to be reflected. I belong to a moment where you make conceptual choices with the scale of an image. We don't know how she might have printed her work for an exhibition, but I imagine it would be a modest size. I look forward to seeing our work in close proximity, for example the dancing ones [*Self-portrait (on sea wall at La Rocquaise)* (1947) and *Dancing in Peckham* (1994, cats 61–2)] and the one of her as a child in the wardrobe and myself at three years old (cats 49–50). I think they could be quite charming juxtapositions. We are different artists, but there is a camaraderie.

SH How has looking at Claude's work in depth affected developments in your own work, in particular on the new work for the exhibition at the National Portrait Gallery? For example, I wonder whether Claude's analogue work has drawn you back to your own early analogue work – I'm thinking about the Polaroids in particular.

GW The fact that we are concentrating on self-portraits for this exhibition has done that, and I have been working in the portrait genre for more than three decades. So it has helped me see my work over a longer period of time. With Claude's work no one knew really where the photographs were destined. We have to make building blocks between her and her photographs, so any explanation of her work is ultimately subjective.

SH How did seeing the original material in the Archive, rather than looking at reproductions, make you think about her work in a different way?

GW It was their minuteness that struck me. They are produced much larger online. Some of her most famous images are impeccably preserved; others are faded – some had been stored in hatboxes.

Fig.26 Wearing looking at La Rocquaise. Photo by Sarah Howgate, 2016

SH You could say the same about some of your own work, such as the rediscovered Polaroids. Obviously, most of your work is kept digitally now, but those early works were kept in boxes.

GW The Polaroids feel like objects to me now – you can't even buy Polaroid film any more; so there is a precious quality about it.

SH The fact that Cahun didn't really exhibit her work in her lifetime, that it was just made for her, and no one else, makes it precious too.

GW I wonder how her work would have been created differently if she had known it was for an exhibition. Some of her images have a sense of the haphazard in them. So we might be looking at things that she was just trying out. I think there'll be developments coming out of this, because I've thought about things that I hadn't considered before, which will definitely move into my work; when I make the new collage for the exhibition.

SH On our research trip to Jersey [fig.20], I feel that you did make a spiritual connection with Claude, especially when we took the photographs in the churchyard [fig.26] and you created *At Claude Cahun's grave* [2015, cat.7]. There was a real sense of a collaborative process.

GW Yes, St Brelade's Bay, where she lived, almost feels preserved in aspic; you sense that you are visiting the past. Now when I think of Claude, I think of Jersey; the two can't be separated. When we were there it felt like there was nothing in the way – it was just her.

SH Yes, it was far more than going to the Archive and looking at her work. It was the whole experience of being in her place.

GW It was amazing to walk in the locations where she photographed some of her self-portraits, such as the beach in front of her house. The research was a bit like method acting, which is an interest of mine, in my films, especially: immersing yourself in someone's life, being in their environment, holding their objects. The more you do that, the more you start finding things. It's almost like I know her, as if she's alive. The more someone is in your head, the more they become a real presence; so she's part of my memory now. All our memories are made up of images, and in my photographic memory there are images of Claude, and she'll always be there and in a bigger way than ever before since I have been working on this with you. She has become part of my family.

SH She's become an additional member of your artistic family.

GW Yes, and I've got even closer to her.

1 Gillian Wearing in exhibition catalogue, Institut Valencià d'Art Modern, 24 September 2015–24 January 2016: 'I no longer know what it must be like to be in the body of a 21 year old, or to have less knowledge than I have now. But I vividly remember being in that damp, dark, rented flat in Earls Court in the early 1980s.'

Claude Cahun's 'self-portraits'

Dawn Ades

The first and only 'self-portrait' photograph of Claude Cahun to be published in her lifetime appeared in the avant-garde journal *Bifur* in 1930 with the title *Frontière humaine* or 'Human Frontier'.[1] This image of Cahun's distorted, elongated and shaved head, on bare shoulders, stripped of all social and sexual attributes, is unequivocally credited to her: 'Phot. Claude Cahun' (fig.27). However, contemporary interviews from the *Chicago Tribune* of 1929 tell a different story, indicating Cahun's partner and stepsister Marcel Moore (pseudonym of Suzanne Malherbe) as the author of the photograph.[2]

The *Chicago Tribute* reports, which give equal billing to Schwob (Cahun's given name) and Moore, were advance publicity for the publication of Cahun's *Aveux non avenus*: 'prose poems on which Mlle Schwob has long been at work ... The volume will probably be illustrated with some extraordinary photographic studies of the author by the artist Moore, her half-sister'.[3] This comment from the interview with Cahun was confirmed by the *Chicago Tribune*'s companion piece, on 'Suzanne Moore', which describes her paintings, illustrations and posters, adding: 'At present the artist is engaged in making a series of distorted photographs of her sister, which probably will be used to illustrate the volume *Aveux non avenus*. ... Entirely printed by herself, these photographs are something quite new in the field.' It is possible but unlikely that the reporter is referring to the photomontages that accompanied *Aveux non*

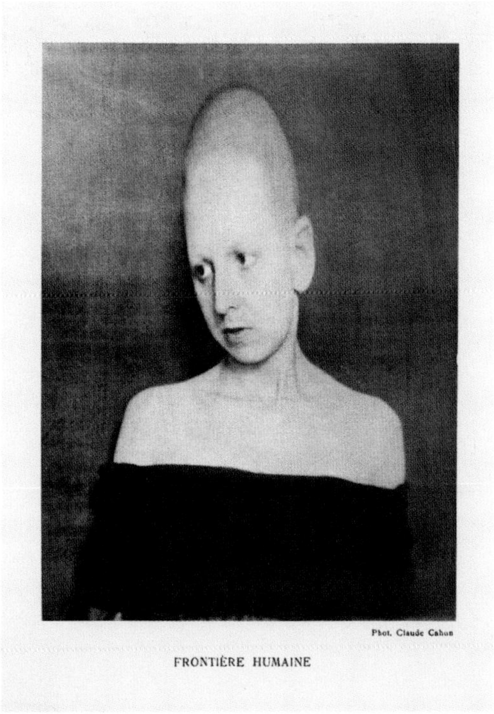

Fig.27 *Self-portrait* by Claude Cahun.
Published in the journal *Bifur*, no.5, April 1930

Fig.28 Window at José Corti bookshop at the launch of *Aveux non avenus*, June 1930

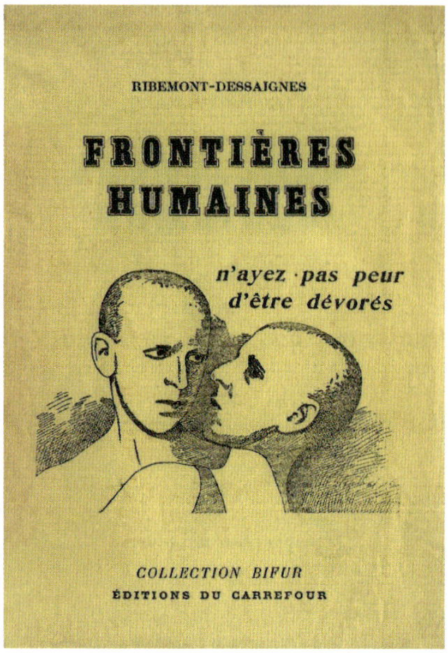

Fig.29 *Frontières humaines* cover (1929) edited by Georges Ribemont-Dessaignes with the work *What do you want from me?*

avenus (1930), one of which was signed 'Moore'. The description of distorted photographs, the comment that they were being made and printed by Moore herself and that they were quite new in the field points to the series of which the *Bifur* photographic portrait was one. The distorted head was 'something quite new', which by then photomontage was not, as striking and original as the photomontages in *Aveux non avenus* none the less are. So here is a conundrum. Why was Cahun credited with a photograph taken by Moore? Why were no more of the 'self-portraits' published? Were they ever intended for public display? What was their relationship to the work and life of Cahun and of Moore? And how did Cahun come to be identified primarily with the 'self-portraits', when in her lifetime she was better known as a writer?

To some of these questions there are so far no definitive answers. Although many of the photographs appear as fragments in the photomontages for *Aveux non avenus*, they must have been more than raw material. It is a problem to call them 'self-portraits' without qualification.[4] They were not taken by Cahun, nor by anonymous accomplices, assistants pressing the button, nor with a delayed-action shutter, but by her partner, Marcel Moore, in a collaborative process with Cahun, of whose complexities one gets some idea from *Aveux non avenus*.[5] This is, as reported in the *Chicago Tribune*, a prose poem, but it is more than that: it includes dreams, letters, confessions, speculations, streams of consciousness, philosophical interludes, poetry, scenarios, *pensées*, comments on myths, such as that of Narcissus, and a constant interchange of characters that have parallels with the theatrical *mises-*

en-scène in the photographs, an essential element in her continual questioning of identity, of desire, of relationships: 'I provide the theatre, you choose your stage sets, your adventures, your character, your sex, your make-up.'[6] To whom does she speak? Or who is speaking? The interrelationship between herself and another, or others of her own selves, is a constant kaleidoscope. Little has come to light about the making of the photographs; Moore's role has to be acknowledged, and the 'Claude Cahun' of the 'self-portraits' was a collaborative creation, as the *Bifur* episode indicates. They were made in the context of play and mutual desire, in which paradox and masquerade took a major part, but were they intended for public consumption?[7] One of the most alluring of the 'self-portraits', *Self-portrait (reflected image in mirror with chequered jacket)*, (1927, cat.68) (which had a companion portrait of Marcel Moore in a comparable position), did make a public appearance, prominently placed in the window display for the launch of *Aveux non avenus* in 1930 (fig.28).

The imminent publication of *Aveux non avenus* probably prompted the publication of the *Bifur* photograph, which was further tied into the *Bifur* milieu by the title, which alludes to the recent publication of *Frontières humaines* (1929) by *Bifur*'s editor Georges Ribemont-Dessaignes. The cover of *Frontières humaines* (fig.29) was a drawing of a double self-portrait *Que me veux-tu? (What do you want from me?)* (1929),[8] adapted from the same series of photographs (fig.10). Cahun and Moore were, apparently, valued members of this milieu, both as writers and artists. Ribemont-Dessaignes had been a member of Paris Dada, closer to Francis Picabia than André Breton, but now definitively detached from the Surrealists.[9] *Bifur* was an eclectic journal, publishing the work of 'independent' writers and artists of the left, including photographs by the new generation of avant-garde photographers like André Kertész, Eli Lotar, Maurice Tabard and Germaine Krull. 'We started out on a new route, the very one that would later be called committed. Literature, certainly, but not gratuitous. No automatic writing either unless something more precisely human comes out of it.'[10] The rejection of automatic writing was an evident reference to Surrealism, and Cahun's close association with *Bifur* (which Breton described as a remarkable dustbin) may be one of the reasons for her relatively tardy affiliation with Surrealism in late 1932.

Surrealism had been launched with the first *Manifesto* by André Breton in 1924, foregrounding the ideas of Sigmund Freud, who had invested dreams with a new value, as throwing light on the workings of the unconscious mind. The *Manifesto* presented automatism as an active route to explore the hidden regions of the psyche, as well as dream narratives, but emphasised that no rules were set as to how to pursue this enterprise, which was primarily concerned with language and poetry. Visual artists were mentioned only in a footnote. By 1929, Surrealism had become, as German–Jewish philosopher and cultural theorist Walter Benjamin noted in his essay 'Surrealism: The Latest Snapshot of the European Intelligentsia', the powerhouse of intellectual and cultural life. Given its ambition to operate on every front of human activity, Surrealism had become increasingly engaged in the cultural wing of political debate; several members, including Breton, joined the French Communist Party (PCF), and there were bitter struggles over aesthetic as well as political issues. One of the paradoxes of Surrealism is that it became famous internationally as an art movement in the 1930s just as it became almost totally isolated politically, rejecting both the capitalist society in which it lived and the now compromised Stalinist Communist Party. This was the situation when Cahun and Moore joined.

None of the 'self-portraits' was exhibited or published in the context of Surrealism, and Cahun's only visual manifestation while a member of the group were the objects she made, and sometimes photographed, with Moore. It was as a writer and activist that she joined the movement, and after she withdrew to Jersey, in 1937, she was almost forgotten.

The forgetting of Claude Cahun was as curious as her rediscovery. One of the first steps in this direction was her inclusion in the exhibition *L'Amour fou: Photography & Surrealism* in 1985. The biographical details in that catalogue were unreliable – they stated that she died in a concentration camp – but at least didn't assume Claude Cahun was a man, as some did at the time.[11] The exhibition had the effect of positioning her in the field of photography, in the context of Surrealism. Over the last few decades, since the photographs resurfaced in the mid-1980s, she has become one of the most influential and esteemed of twentieth-century artists, her work appealing in succession to feminists, to postmodernists and to conceptual artists; its radical questioning of identity and performative use of photography remaining a live and inexhaustible source of inspiration and reference. It has not, in other words, remained fixed in one historical moment, and as a corollary to this its genesis and context have retained a degree of mystery. How far the two may be linked is an interesting question. Because so little of her and Marcel Moore's collaborative visual work was made public at the time, and the conditions of its production are so obscure, there has been no chain linking it back to a specific moment in the history of photography. As Katharine Conley wrote of *Héroïnes*, texts that remained unpublished as a whole until long after Cahun's death, they may become as canonical as the (also unpublished) 'self-portraits' because 'they hide ... as much as they reveal and speak to us as much of our own time as hers'.[12]

There are good reasons for her work speaking to us more than half a century later; what is trickier to explain is why she was forgotten after the Second World War. She was omitted from historical exhibitions of Surrealism, when this genre got going in the 1960s, having slipped from

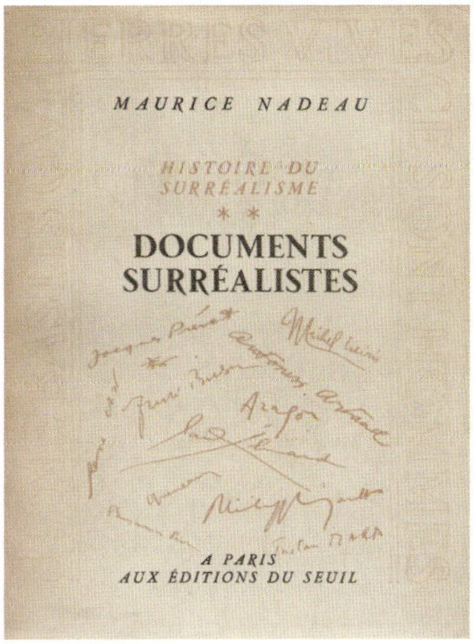

Fig.30 *Documents Surréalistes*
by Maurice Nadeau, 1948

the collective memory of the group and being without, for its historians, a clear identity. Although she exhibited once with the Surrealists, at the time she was not thought of as a visual artist but as a writer and political activist. This, too, was how she apparently thought of herself. In a document drawn up in Jersey after 1945, she refers to her activity during the Occupation as the logical continuation of her 'activity as a writer in France at the time of the Popular Front'.[13] This goes some way to explaining her absence from the Surrealist exhibitions of the 1960s and 1970s (along with many other women artists).

By 1945 she had become a marginal figure; for Maurice Nadeau in *Histoire du Surréalisme* (1964) she is more of a fellow-traveller than a member. He only names her among the signatories of the 1935 Contre-attaque *Manifesto* (pages 180–1), which 'was signed not only by Breton, Eluard, Pastoureau, Péret, but also by former surrealists like Boiffard, by sympathisers like Claude Cahun, Maurice Heine, by intellectuals like the actor Roger Blin, P. Aimer etc., and by Breton's former enemy Georges Bataille, mainspring of the [Contre-attaque] movement'.[14] Part of her tract *Les Paris sont ouverts* ('It's anyone's guess how it will end') (1934) was included in Nadeau's selection of pamphlets and manifestos, *Documents Surréalistes* (1948, fig.30), and it was this that her biographer François Leperlier came across in 1968, during the student uprisings in Paris.

> The affirmation of an active, extreme left wing seeking an organic liaison with the working-class movements, the preference given to the cultural stakes, to the critique of everyday life, to the invention of new forms of action, to the lyrical adventure … I recognised there, even in the choice of turns of phrase (the Marxist-Leninist

vocabulary had, thirty-five years on, recovered some of its colour), a purpose that seemed to respond to the demands of the moment.[15]

From this discovery of a voice that chimed with the revolutionary movements of 1968, Leperlier recovered her lost history. He traces her passage – as what he calls a *funambule* or 'tightrope walker' – from her symbolist origins through the different avant-garde and modernist groups in Paris, often at odds with each other, to her affiliation with Surrealism. She was a gifted actor and was as engaged in the assumption of different roles in private as she was in public on stage. Linked to the theatre are the photographs of her as a silk-clad Buddha, sitting cross-legged in symmetrical ritual pose (cat.46). She belonged to the Union des Amis des Arts Esotériques (Union of the Friends of Esoteric Arts), which, from about 1923, held soirées in a private theatre, including music, poetry recitations and dance, 'whose proceedings were determinedly symbolist and spiritualist'.[16]

She and Marcel Moore joined the Association des écrivains et artistes révolutionnaires (AEAR) at the end of 1932, and it was in this context that she met Breton and the Surrealists. The first tract she signed with the Surrealists was 'Protestez!' (March 1933), which violently opposed the recent fascist takeover in Germany and also attacked French imperialism. She engaged immediately in the ideological combat over the question of the role of writers and poets in a revolutionary organisation; fully in agreement with the Surrealists' position, she wrote a short piece on poetry for the literary section of the AEAR, and when Breton was excluded from the organisation in July 1933, followed by the rest of the Surrealists, expanded it into the polemical pamphlet *Les Paris sont ouverts*. The rupture was inevitable as the Surrealists could not accept the principle of a proletarian literature and persisted in maintaining their independence at a time when the Communist Party (CP) was hardening in its embrace of socialist realism. Breton had already been in trouble for publishing an erotic (if not pornographic) text by Salvador Dalí in *Le Surréalisme au service de la révolution,* and the immediate cause for his exclusion was the publication of a letter by the French writer and philosopher Ferdinand Alquié criticising a Soviet film. Breton later said: 'Anyone looking for a truly evocative image of that epoch would find it in a brochure published in 1934 by Claude Cahun with the title *Les Paris sont ouverts.*'[17] Maintaining, like Breton in *Légitime défense* and *Misère de la poésie*, the right to freedom of expression, and attacking both poetry-propaganda and the stale pursuit of aesthetic rules (the *métier* of poet), she ends: 'Only indirect action seems to me efficacious, both from the point of view of propaganda and from the point of view of poetry.'[18]

Throughout this period Cahun hosted long debates in her studio concerning the articulation of poetic experience and political engagement, and also eroticism. She and Moore were involved in one of the most extreme attempts by intellectuals to take revolutionary action and convert individual experience to collective action: Contre-attaque, which lasted from September 1935 to March 1936. The organisation took the form of two secret societies, one on the Right Bank ('Sade'), the other on the Left Bank ('Marat', to which Cahun and Moore belonged); a manifesto and five collective declarations were published, and there were frequent meetings. But the disproportion between the extreme gravity of the international and national situation, with the rise of fascism and the Stalinisation of the CP, and the hyperbolic assertions of a small group of intellectuals inevitably led to its collapse. The failure of Contre-attaque and the political instability in France may have contributed to Cahun's withdrawal to Jersey in 1937, where she lived with Moore to the end of her life. She did join the Fédération Internationale de l'art révolutionnaire indépendant (FIARI) in 1939, but otherwise took no further public action with the Surrealists.[19]

However, it was not coincidental that one of the most fruitful and radical Surrealist interventions reached its height in the mid-1930s: the 'Surrealist object'. As Steven Harris has argued, this was the time of maximum resistance by the Surrealists to the idea of art and the *métier*.[20] The Surrealist object was in a sense the triumph of the supersession of art. Salvador Dalí's text on 'Objets surréalistes' (1931) had galvanised the group – writers as well as artists – to fabricate objects constructed from familiar day-to-day materials but geared to sexually symbolic meanings and liable to generate a frisson of erotic excitement in the viewer. He was picking up on an earlier proposition of Breton's, that objects that had appeared in dreams could be fabricated and put into circulation among the utilitarian things that surround us, thereby sowing confusion and throwing discredit on those 'things of 'reason'.[21] They thus would function like, but would not be, works of art. The *Exposition surréaliste d'objets* (22–9 May 1936) at Galerie Charles Ratton in Paris contained an astonishing array of objects of all kinds: found, natural, interpreted, ready-made. Cahun showed three objects, although only two were named in the catalogue: *Un air de famille* and *Souris valseuses* (both c.1936). She and Moore had previously fabricated and photographed little ephemeral constructions, such as *Entre nous* (c.1930, cat.35) or *Le Père* (1932), several of which appeared as illustrations to Lise Deharme's book of poems for children *Le Coeur de Pic* (1937). Cahun also contributed an important text to the special issue of *Cahiers d'art* on the Object, 'Prenez garde aux objets domestiques':

> I insist on a primary truth: one has to discover, handle, *tame*, fabricate irrational objects oneself in order to appreciate the particular or general value of those before our eyes. That is why, in some respects, *manual* workers would be better placed than intellectuals to grasp

> their meaning, did not everything in capitalist society, including communist propaganda, turn them away from it.[22]

The third object, however, did survive: a tennis ball painted to resemble a human eye, but vertical and surrounded with pubic hair, with a cut-out cloud shape behind and a small wooden hand beside it (fig.11). Two phrases are inscribed on its base: 'La Marseillaise est un chant révolutionnaire. La loi punit le contrefacteur des Travaux forcés' [The Marseillaise is a revolutionary song. The law punishes the forger with hard labour]. Like Alberto Giacometti's sculpture *Suspended Ball* (1931), the object is both erotic and violent, and ambiguous gender-wise – both phallic and female. Harris has analysed in detail the ways Cahun draws on Georges Bataille's novella *Histoire de l'oeil* (1928) and Luis Buñuel and Salvador Dalí's film *Un Chien andalou* (1929), with the famous opening scene of the slitting of an eye (fig.31), its relationship to the fetish and to both Freudian and Marxist theory. He explains the two phrases convincingly as references to the betrayal of socialist principles by the Popular Front government in France.[23]

But if her objects figured publicly in Surrealism, the 'self-portrait' photographs did not. It may seem surprising that they were not seen in the light of the Surrealists' interrogation of the self, expressed most famously in Breton's opening lines in *Nadja*: 'Who am I? If this once I were to rely on a proverb, then perhaps everything would amount to knowing whom I "haunt".'[24] This opens up a search for the other, in Breton's case, invariably, a woman. In addition he believed in an ideal transparency in the relation between life and art, experience and expression, as he described in *L'Amour fou*: 'The house I live in, my life, what I write: I dream that these appear from afar as these cubes of crystal salt appear close to.'[25]

It was probably the theatrical side of Cahun's multiple personae in the 'self-portraits' as much as the lesbianism that jarred and prevented them from finding a platform, although they are fully consonant with Surrealism. When Cahun finally joined forces with the Surrealist group, her reception was, for her, something of a disappointment. In the early months of frequenting the Surrealist café, she would arrive in costume.

> This was a milieu that she was keen to impress, to seduce, and to hold back from at the same time, a milieu that she absolutely wanted to privilege and that intimidated her, where she imagined that she could freely explore her 'self-staging' ... Her *entrances*, as a couple with Suzanne, hair close-cropped, coloured pink or gold, with expressionist make-up, wearing eccentric gowns or even male suits, and a monocle, did not pass unnoticed and were not to everyone's taste.[26]

Her appearances at the group meetings, dressed up as a male dandy, or with pink or gold hair – probably her cropped hair in the mirror

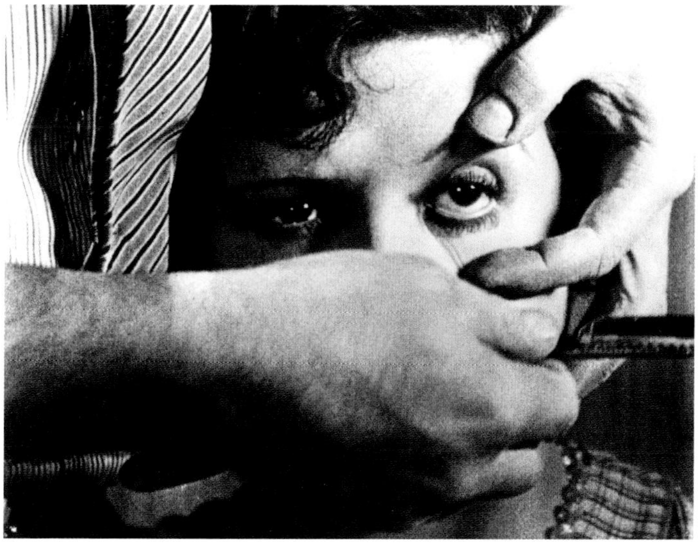

Fig.31 Still from Buñuel and Dalí's film *Un Chien andalou*, 1929

photograph (cat.68) is gold – disturbed and irritated some of the Surrealists, Breton especially, for whom this was too theatrical, fanciful and frankly homosexual. These guises were those that are registered in the 'self-portraits', and the fact that she appeared in public in the same manner suggests that the 'self-portraits' were not simply a private affair. (However, at the International Surrealist Exhibition in London in 1936, she does appear in a group photo wearing a demure summer dress. The photograph was cropped (perhaps by her) to exclude her (fig.32).)

The 'self-portrait' in *Bifur* stands out even in a journal that made a feature of contemporary photography. It is disturbing not because it is an optical puzzle, like images produced by close-ups and high-angle photographs, but because the subject hardly looks human. It is on the frontier of what 'being human' might mean, stripped of all social and sexual attributes. No cue as to gender is given by the severe black binding round the torso, which has the effect of isolating the head and shoulders, as if it were a classical bust. This deliberate clash of genres – the mock-classical bust in contradistinction to the not-quite human of the elongated head – is characteristic of Cahun/Moore's subtle and complex approach. Inscribed on one of the photomontages for *Aveux non avenus* is the phrase: 'Under this mask another mask. I will never finish removing all these faces.' [ch. 1X] The *Bifur* 'self-portrait' is almost as though she has succeeded, and we are witnessing the end of a process of stripping down to an 'ur' head. 'A proposition for Lent: everyone who wears a mask the rest of the year should come out bare-faced, unrecognisable.'[27] The notion of 'bare-faced' and thus 'unrecognisable' seems to be probing into the territory famously analysed by Joan Rivière, who argued in a text often mentioned in connection with Cahun, and published just before the *Bifur* portrait, that there is no such thing as

Fig.32 Surrealists in London, 1936: (left to right) E.L.T. Mesens, Roland Penrose, André Breton, David Gascoyne and Claude Cahun

an essential feminine identity but that 'Womanliness is a masquerade'.[28] However, masquerade for Cahun was not to do with womanliness. It has been suggested that the elongated head could be given a Freudian reading, as a 'phallic projection'.[29] Seen thus, Cahun could be playing with the idea of the phallic woman, presenting herself as a lesbian in defiance of the male gaze. Leperlier describes her as 'a young woman who was beautiful but who went out of her way sometimes to debase herself, sometimes to sublimate herself, as if it was always a question of challenging both her own femininity and the virile look which could be attached to it'.[30] How does this need to reject both her own femininity and the virile look that would accompany it manifest itself?

In *Aveux non avenus,* Cahun wrote: 'Masculine? Feminine? It depends on the situation. Neuter is the only gender that always suits me.'[31] Neuter as no-gender, what is now referred to as non-binary, rather than both genders, as with the hermaphrodite. This is a key statement, far ahead of its time, illuminating some of her most iconic images. Consider, for instance, her portrait dressed as a dandy (fig.33), in the manner of famous lesbians of the time, like her friend Sylvia Beach or Romaine Brooks, in a black suit, hand on hip, a white handkerchief in her top pocket and a shaved head. Although in male guise, she does not look like a woman adopting masculine attire, becoming a masculine woman: it is more as if from a neutral position she resolutely remains unaligned.

The innate ability of the photograph to present a real image of a totally fictitious nature has been fundamental for artists engaged in the testing of identity in a number of different contexts. Contemporaneously with Cahun, Marcel Duchamp exploited it with the connivance of Man

Ray in the creation of his female *alter ego*, Rrose Sélavy (fig.13). The photographic portraits of both Cahun and Duchamp resonate with generations of post-war artists, sometimes consciously, but sometimes the connection is only recognised in retrospect. A comparison with the American artist Martha Wilson is interesting (fig.34). Wilson changed herself into a man and then a man in drag, masquerading as a woman, in a double denial of a fixed female identity. However, these double reversals are still operating in the binary-gender field, whereas Cahun challenges it.

Other bold, confrontational work in the 1970s by artists like Carolee Schneemann, Lynda Benglis and Adrian Piper, often involving performance, dug into female identity and turned it inside out. Performing to the camera was an important aspect of the work of these artists but, as Lucy Lippard pointed out, 'Claude Cahun was totally unknown to all of us at the time.'[32]

A work of art has the right to a life beyond and different from that for which it was originally made. But, as the American feminist art historian Whitney Chadwick warned, there is a need, in the case of Cahun's 'self-portraits', to understand their complex origins and authorship.

> The neatness with which Cahun's photographs have been annexed to postmodern concerns with the decentered subject and with identity

Fig.33 *Self-portrait (as a dandy, three-quarter length)* by Claude Cahun, 1921–2

as contingent and mutable has obscured the complexity and contradictions of her writings and blinded many to the works' representations of conflicted identities.[33]

What are now presented as the 'self-portraits' of 'Claude Cahun' were the result of a collaborative practice at the deepest level between artistic partners and lovers. They exist in a kind of *terrain vague* between portrait and self-portrait, in the context of masquerades and scenarios, devised by them both for Cahun and enacted by her. They are, in a sense, an extension of their life together, and there is continuity between them, the objects and photographs of the objects, and the writings, which blurs the distinction between private and public, life and work, writing and the image. Cahun claimed later in life that she had always been a Surrealist: 'In my life as a whole, I am what I have always been (my earliest memories of childhood bear witness): *surréaliste*. Essentially. At least as far as one can be without killing oneself or being put in an asylum.'[34]

Fig.34 *Posturing: Drag* by Martha Wilson, 1972/96
Photograph by Doug Waterman

All translations by Dawn Ades unless otherwise stated.

1 *Bifur,* no.5, April 1930.

2 A so-called self-portrait of Claude Cahun, c.1911, shows the young writer in the guise of the beautiful ballet dancer Cléo de Mérode; this was about the time she met Malherbe and may be one of the first examples of their photographic collaboration.

3 News cutting from the *Chicago Tribune*, European edition, of an article by Golda M. Goldman, 'Who's Who Abroad: Lucie Schwob and Suzanne Moore [sic]', 1929, JHT/2003/00001/109 and reproduced in *Don't Kiss Me: The Art of Claude Cahun and Marcel Moore,* ed. Louise Downie (Tate, London, 2016; in association with Jersey Heritage Trust), p.226.

4 Among those who have called for greater recognition for Moore is Tirza True Latimer; see her essay 'Acting Out: Claude Cahun and Marcel Moore' in *Don't Kiss Me*, op. cit.

5 The English translation of *Aveux non avenus* by Susan de Muth proposed two titles, *Disavowals or Cancelled Confessions* (Tate, London, 2007). All translations are from this edition, but the French title is given here.

6 *Aveux*, p.127.

7 Studies examining the specifically lesbian nature of the 'self-portraits' include Abigail Solomon-Godeau, 'The Equivocal "I": Claude Cahun as Lesbian Subject', *Inverted Odysseys: Claude Cahun, Maya Deren, Cindy Sherman*, ed. Shelley Rice, exh. cat. (The MIT Press, Cambridge (Massachusetts) and London, 1999); Julie Cole 'Claude Cahun, Marcel Moore and the Collaborative Construction of a Lesbian Subjectivity', *Reclaiming Female Agency*, ed. Norma Broude and Mary D. Garrard (University of California, 2005).

8 The style of the drawing suggests it is by Marcel Moore.

9 In 1930 he signed the pamphlet *Un Cadavre*, attacking Breton.

10 Georges Ribemont-Dessaignes, *Déjà jadis*, quoted in François Leperlier, *Claude Cahun: L'écart et la métamorphose* (Jean-Michel Place, Paris, 1992), p.119.

11 Rosalind Krauss and Jane Livingstone, with Dawn Ades, *L'Amour fou: Photography & Surrealism*, exh. cat. (Abbeville Press and Corcoran Gallery of Art, 1985; Arts Council of Great Britain, 1986).

12 Katharine Conley, 'Claude Cahun's Counter-archival Héroïnes', *Don't Kiss Me*, p.24.

13 Leperlier, p.268.

14 Maurice Nadeau, *History of Surrealism*, trans. Richard Howard (Cape, London, 1968), p.196.

15 Leperlier, p.168.

16 Leperlier, p.89.

17 André Breton, *Entretiens* (Nouvelle Revue Française, Paris, 1952), p.169.

18 Claude Cahun, *Ecrits*, ed. François Leperlier (Jean-Michel Place, Paris, 2002), p.515.

19 Fédération Internationale de l'art révolutionnaire indépendant. Her adhesion was announced in the FIARI bulletin *Clé*, no.1 (January 1939). Its manifesto was drawn up by Breton and Leon Trotsky, but signed by Breton and Diego Rivera.

20 Steven Harris, *Surrealist Art and Thought in the 1930s: Art, Politics and the Psyche* (Cambridge University Press, Cambridge, 2004).

21 André Breton, 'Introduction to the Discourse on the Paucity of Reality' (1924, published 1925) in *What is Surrealism? Selected Writings*, ed. Franklin Rosemont (Pluto Press, London, 1978) p.26.

22 Claude Cahun, 'Prenez garde aux objets domestiques', *Cahiers d'art* (1936), p.46. Translated by Steven Harris.

23 Steven Harris, 'Coup d'oeil', *Oxford Art Journal* (vol.24, 2001).

24 André Breton, *Nadja* (1928), trans. Richard Howard (Penguin, London, 1960).

25 André Breton *L'Amour fou* (1937), p.14. The first part of *L'Amour fou* appeared as 'La beauté sera convulsive' in the Surrealist journal *Minotaure* in 1934.

26 Leperlier, p.161.

27 *Aveux*, p.127.

28 Joan Rivière, 'Womanliness as a masquerade', *International Journal of Psychoanalysis,* 10 (1929), pp.303–13.

29 Cole, p.354.

30 Leperlier, p.161.

31 *Aveux,* p.151. Cahun translated writings by Havelock Ellis, the British physician and social reformer who studied sexual behaviour, wrote *Studies in the Psychology of Sex* (1897–1928) and campaigned against the social stigma attached to homosexuality, which he suggested could be a third sex.

32 Lucy Lippard, 'Scattering Selves', *Inverted Odysseys*, op. cit., p.32.

33 Whitney Chadwick, 'An Infinite Play of Empty Mirrors: Women, Surrealism, and Self-representation', *Mirror Images*, ed. Whitney Chadwick (The MIT Press, Cambridge (Massachusetts) and London, 1998), p.7.

34 Letter to Jean Schuster, 19 February 1953: Leperlier, p.157.

Claude Cahun: chronology

Tanya Bentley

1894 Born 25 October at 6 rue du Calvaire in Nantes as Lucy Renée Mathilde Schwob, daughter of Maurice Schwob, owner and director of the Nantes regional newspaper *Le Phare de la Loire*, and Victorine Marie Courbebaisse. She is the niece of the Symbolist writer Marcel Schwob and great-niece of Léon Cahun, traveller, novelist and later conservator for the Bibliothèque Mazarine in Paris.

1895–1905 While her mother is regularly hospitalised because of struggles with her mental health, Lucy lives mainly with her paternal grandmother, Mathilde Cahun, in her apartment in cours Cambronne in central Nantes.

1906–8 During the second examination of the Dreyfus Affair in 1906,[1] Lucy is taken out of her lycée in Nantes after she is subjected to anti-Semitic acts by fellow classmates. For the next two years, she continues her studies in an English boarding school in Surrey.

1909 Lucy returns to her lycée in Nantes, participating in some classes while also receiving private tuition. She meets Suzanne Malherbe (1892–1972, fig.35), another student at the school, who would become her lifelong friend and partner.

1909–13 Escalation of Lucy's long-standing health problems; she displays suicidal tendencies and is diagnosed with anorexia.

1914–16 Lucy publishes her first article 'Vues et visions' in 1914 in the French literary magazine *Mercure de France*, under the pseudonym Claude Courlis, and writes the semi-biographical texts 'Les Jeux uraniens' (fig.36), marking the first time she uses her enduring pseudonym Claude Cahun, adopting a gender-neutral forename and the surname of her paternal lineage. Cahun and Marcel Moore (pseudonym of Suzanne Malherbe) begin their artistic collaborations around this period. Cahun registers to study literature and philosophy at the University of the Sorbonne in Paris.

1917 Having divorced Cahun's mother, Maurice Schwob, Cahun's father, marries Moore's widowed mother, Marie-Eugénie Malherbe, and they move to an apartment on the top floor of the *Le Phare* office building at place du Commerce, Nantes.

1918–21 Cahun continues her literary career and is a regular contributor to Albert Gavy-Bélédin's paper, *La Gerbe*, under pseudonyms Claude Cahun and Daniel Douglas. Cahun stays in Paris for long periods at a time, frequenting Adrienne Monnier's bookshop, La Maison des Amis des Livres. Cahun decides to shave her head.

Fig.35 Suzanne Malherbe by Claude Cahun, 1915

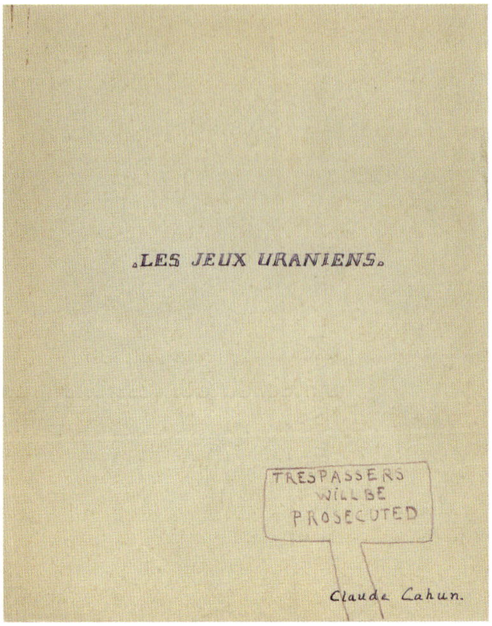

„LES JEUX URANIENS„

TRESPASSERS
WILL BE
PROSECUTED

Claude Cahun.

Fig.36 'Les Jeux uraniens' manuscript by Claude Cahun, 1914

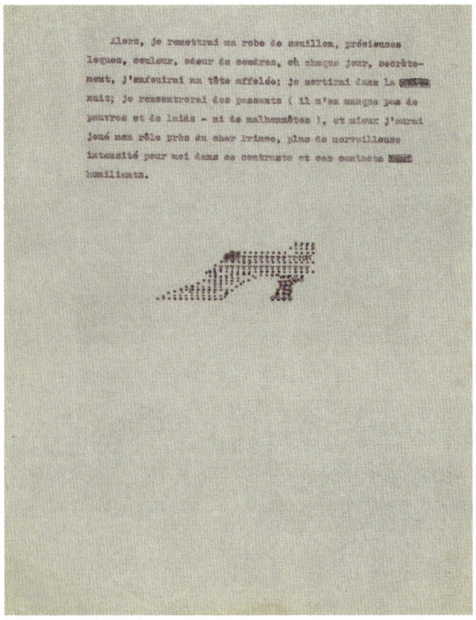

Alors, je remettrai ma robe de souillon, précieuses loques, couleur, odeur de cendres, et chaque jour, secrètement, j'enfouirai ma tête affolée; je sortirai dans la nuit; je rencontrerai des passants (il n'en manque pas de pauvres et de laids – ni de malhonnêtes), et mieux j'aurai joué mon rôle près du cher Prince, plus de merveilleuse intensité pour moi dans ce contraste et ces contacts humiliants.

Fig.37 *Héroïnes* manuscript with *Cinderella slipper*, decorated with typewriter keys, 1925

Fig.38 Claude Cahun in her Paris apartment, 70 bis rue Notre-Dame-des-Champs, 1923

1922–4 Cahun and Moore move from Nantes to Montparnasse, Paris (fig.38). Cahun's literary activity slows as her interest turns towards theatre and performance. She is a founding member of L'Union des Amis des Arts Ésotériques in 1923.

1925–31 Cahun returns to writing and in 1925 publishes in two separate journals the majority of *Héroïnes,* a collection of monologues by misunderstood fairy-tale and biblical heroines (fig.37). This period culminates in the publication by Éditions du Carrefour of *Aveux non avenus* in 1930 (translated into English by Susan de Muth as *Disavowals or Cancelled Confessions* (Tate, 2007)). It is published with ten complex photomontages created collaboratively with Moore (page 56). When the book was launched, Cahun and Moore held a mini-exhibition in a bookshop window (fig.41). Death of Cahun's father, Maurice Schwob, in 1928. • In the late 1920s, Cahun's photographic activity intensifies. She produces the 'In training' series, costumed in boxer shorts, painted lips and a provocative leotard with paste-on nipples (cats 2–5), and a series wearing a robe decorated with masks (cat.53 and fig.15). In 1929, Cahun's theatrical performances for theatre company Le Plateau as 'Le Diable' (Satan) in *Le Mystère d'Adam* (cat.64) and 'Monsieur de la Première Table' in the satire *Banlieu* (cat.63) as well as her critically acclaimed performance as 'Elle' in *Barbe-Bleue* (cat.65 and fig.18) are well documented in photographs by Moore. In 1930, the only photographic self-portrait of Cahun to be published in her lifetime features in *Bifur*, a journal edited by Georges Ribemont-Dessaignes (fig.27).

1932–6 In April 1932, Cahun is introduced to André Breton by writer and screenwriter, Jacques Viot, marking the start of her work with the Surrealists. During this period, Cahun becomes increasingly involved with politics, participating in Surrealist demonstrations. This culminates in the publication in 1934 of the political pamphlet *Les Paris sont ouverts* ('It's anyone's guess how it will end'), in which she expresses her belief in the political potential of art and poetry for everyone. In 1935, she joins Breton's new left-leaning group, Contre-attaque, signing a statement from the Surrealists in July that reused as its title the words of French revolutionary, Maximilien Robespierre: 'Il n'y a pas de liberté pour les ennemis de la liberté' ('There is no freedom for the enemies of freedom'). Her involvement with Surrealism prompts further artworks that comprise assemblages of objects (cat.35 and fig.11). In 1936, Cahun participates in the Surrealist exhibition at the Galerie Charles Ratton, Paris, and visits the International Surrealist Exhibition at the New Burlington Galleries, London.

1937–9 In March 1937, Cahun and Moore leave Paris for the island of Jersey, with which they are familiar from family holidays. In July they acquire La Rocquaise (fig.39), a neglected house in St Brelade's Bay. They live a remote life, continuing their photographic collaborations.

1940–4 On 1 July 1940, Jersey is invaded by German forces. Schwob and Malherbe (they revert to using their given names) remain in Jersey. They produce counter-propaganda tracts in active resistance of the Occupation. Malherbe translates news broadcasts on BBC Radio, which Schwob converts into short, catchy text. Tracts are signed by 'der Soldat ohne Namen' ('the soldier with no name'), in an attempt to create the illusion of resistance within the German army (fig.40). Schwob and Malherbe are arrested on 25 July 1944. On 16 November they are sentenced to death, as Malherbe describes: 'for propaganda undermining the morale of the German forces', 'to six years' penal servitude for listening to the BBC' and 'six months for having arms and a camera'.[2] Although they are determined to face the charge, the sentence is dropped the following February.

1945–53 Jersey is liberated on 9 May 1945, and Cahun and Moore are released from prison. They move back to La Rocquaise and return to photography, producing a defiant portrait, taken in May 1945, showing Cahun gripping a Nazi eagle insignia between her teeth (cat.80); a post-Liberation series in 1947, of Cahun dancing along a concrete wall (cat.62); and in c.1948 the series *Le chemin des chats*, of Cahun led blindfolded by a cat (cat.82). In January 1951, Cahun receives the Médaille de la Reconnaissance française (Medal of French Gratitude) for her acts of resistance during the Second World War. She makes her final visit to Paris in June 1953, meeting up once again with Breton.

1954 Cahun dies at the age of sixty on 8 December in St Helier hospital, Jersey. Moore buries Cahun in St Brelade's church cemetery.

1972 Moore commits suicide in Jersey on 19 February.

In 1995 and 2003, the Jersey Heritage Trust acquired a vast archive of Cahun and Moore's work, including photographs, drawings and manuscripts. Cahun has been the subject of a number of retrospectives, including: *Claude Cahun Photographe*, Musée d'Art Moderne de la Ville de Paris (1995), *Claude Cahun*, Institut Valencià d'Art Modern (2001–2002) and *Claude Cahun*, Jeu de Paume, Paris (2011).

1 The Dreyfus Affair (1894–1906) was a political scandal that divided France over the false accusation against Jewish officer Alfred Dreyfus of spying for the Germans. In 1898, novelist Emile Zola famously accused French officers of discrimination in an open letter to the President entitled 'J'Accuse!'.

2 *Jersey Evening Post*, 30 June 1945, p.4.

Fig.39 Claude Cahun in the doorway at La Rocquaise, after 1937

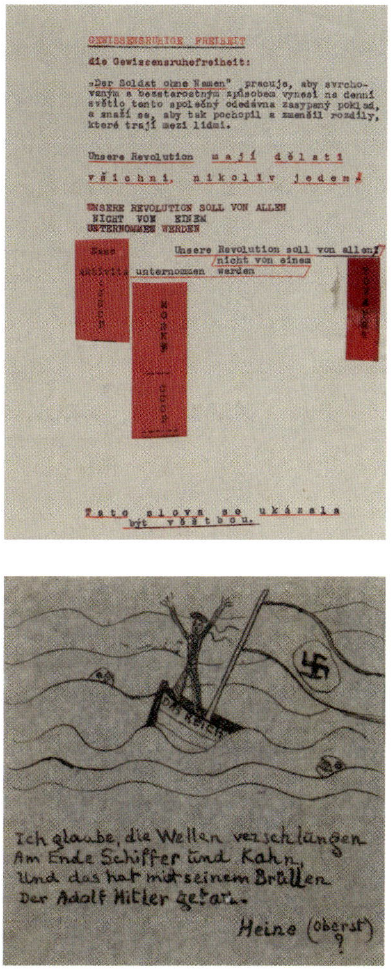

Fig 40 Propaganda leaflets made by Cahun and Moore during the German Occupation of Jersey, 1940–4

Fig.41 Claude Cahun (left) with an unidentified woman outside the mini-exhibition held at José Corti bookshop, Paris, for the launch of *Aveux non avenus*, June 1930

Fig.42 Interior at La Rocquaise (one of Cahun and Moore's photomontages can be seen on the wall), after 1937

Gillian Wearing: chronology

Tanya Bentley

Fig.43 Gillian (right) and her friend Michele Markham in Birmingham, 1981

1963–79 Gillian Wearing is born in 1963, in Birmingham, to parents Brian Wearing and Jean Gregory. She has two siblings: a sister, Jane, and brother, Richard. She attends Dartmouth High School and decides against continuing with her art studies in her third year at the school.

1980–90 Wearing leaves school at the age of sixteen and finds work as on office clerk at an insurance broker in Birmingham. Three years later, Wearing settles in London with two friends. She quickly finds secretarial work and attends evening classes at the Sir John Cass School of Art. In 1984, she begins working as a secretary at an animation studio in Soho's Golden Square. This triggers Wearing to apply for a foundation course at Chelsea School of Art in London. She completes her BTech in Art & Design at Chelsea in 1987 and goes on to gain a BA (Hons) in Fine Art at Goldsmiths College, University of London in 1990. • In the late 1980s, Wearing begins to produce Polaroid 'selfies' (cat.24), which gradually document her ageing process. She becomes interested in Surrealism, particularly the work of Salvador Dalí, and makes the self-portrait *Me as a clock* (1990, cat.87).

1991–5 In 1993, Wearing takes part in the UK touring exhibition, *BT Young Contemporaries*, and receives the BT New Contemporaries Award. First solo show, *I'm desperate*, takes places at City Racing gallery in London. • Wearing explores themes of confession and self-exposure in a number of photographic and film projects including: *Signs that say what you want them to say and not signs that say what someone else wants you to say* (1992–3, fig.45); *Take your top off* (1993); *Confess all on video. Don't worry, you will be in disguise. Intrigued? Call Gillian* (1994); *My favourite track* (1994) and *Dancing in Peckham* (1994, cat.61). The last three of these were premiered at Interim Art in London (now Maureen Paley) in 1994. • In 1994, Wearing's *Signs that say* series appears on the front cover of

Fig.44 Wearing in Earl's Court, London, 1984

Fig.45 *Signs that say what you want them to say and not signs that say what someone else wants you to say* by Gillian Wearing, 1992–3

Fig.46 *Observer Magazine*, September 2000

Fig.47 Michael Landy and Gillian Wearing in photo booth with Raphael effect, 2001

Artforum magazine. • In 1995–6, Wearing's work is exhibited in *Brilliant!: new art from London* at the Walker Art Center, Minneapolis, USA: the first major museum to display works from the new generation of British artists.

1996–9 Wins the Turner Prize in 1997 for her colour film, *60 minute silence*, 1996, depicting twenty-six male and female police officers posing in silence. That same year, Wearing creates two films, entitled *10–16* and *2 into 1*, that feature people lip-synching. She wins the Oberhausen Short Film Festival Award in 1998 for the latter film, in which the voices of a mother and her twin sons are lip-synched so that the mother's words come from the sons' mouths and vice versa. Wearing takes part in *Sensation*, at the Royal Academy of Arts, London, in 1997. • She produces *Drunk* (1999), a black-and-white, three-channel video documentary of a group of alcoholics.

2000–2 Wearing has a number of solo exhibitions including: *Gillian Wearing*, Serpentine Gallery, London (2000) and La Caixa, Madrid (2001); *Sous Influence,* Musée d'Art Moderne de la Ville de Paris; *Unspoken,* Kunstverein München, Munich (2001), *Mass Observation,* Museum of Contemporary Art, Chicago (2002), Institute of Contemporary Art, Philadelphia (2003), and Musée d'Art Contemporain de Montréal (2003). • In 2002, Wearing directs an advertisement entitled 'You Never Know' for television and cinema based on her lip-synching work and goes on to win a Gold British Arrows Award (formerly British Television Advertising Awards) for public service advertising. • In 2002, Wearing is made an Honorary Fellow of Goldsmiths College, University of London.

2003–6 The production of a colour video, posing as her grandmother *Nancy Gregory* (2002, cat.93), triggers Wearing's photographic series, 'Family Album' (2003–6), most of which was shown at Maureen Paley in 2003. Wearing's father, Brian Wearing, dies in 2005. • In 2004, Wearing is awarded an Honorary Doctorate by the University for the Creative Arts, based in the south of England. • Wearing continues exploring themes of family dynamics and modern television through her video installation *Family History* (2006), drawing from footage from 1974 BBC fly-on-the-wall documentary series *The Family*. • Her video project *Snapshot* (2005), commissioned for Bloomberg SPACE, London, focuses on the female life cycle and traces the evolution of still portraiture.
A major survey of Wearing's works titled *Living proof* takes place at the Australian Centre for Contemporary Art (ACCA)in Melbourne, 2006.

2007–9 In 2007, Wearing becomes a life member of the Royal Academy of Arts, London. • Further solo exhibitions are shown in the Galleria Civica di Arte Contemporanea, Trento, Italy (2007), where she creates *Family monument*, a public sculpture of a typical Trentino family, and at the

Musée Rodin, Paris (2009), where she presents two videos on the theme of confession.

2010–13 Wearing makes her first full-length film, which merges fiction and documentary film-making and method-acting, entitled *Self Made* (2010). The following year, she organises *People* (2005–11) at Tanya Bonakdar Gallery in New York, a mini-retrospective that includes video installations, photographic portraiture and sculpture. • In 2011, Wearing is awarded an OBE for her contribution to the arts. • A major retrospective of her work is held at the Whitechapel Gallery, London (2012) and Kunstsammlung Nordrhein-Westfalen, Düsseldorf, and then at Museum Brandhorst, Munich (2012–13). Her photograph *Me as Cahun holding a mask of my face* (2012, cat.6) is included in the exhibition. It is part of a series in which she presents herself as her 'Spiritual Family', also featuring herself as Diane Arbus, Robert Mapplethorpe and Andy Warhol (cats 51–2 and 91).

2014–16 In 2014, Wearing unveils her sculpture, *A real Birmingham family* (fig.49), raising questions about what constitutes a twenty-first-century family. That year, Wearing is also nominated for the Human Rights Art Award and The Vincent Award, in which she enters her work *Me as an artist in 1984* (cat.23). She exhibits *My fortune and misfortune* (cats 33–4), lifelike casts of her hands, and two new video works, *We are here* (2014), in which residents from the West Midlands present a series of posthumous monologues about regrets and losses from their lifetime, and *Fear and loathing* (2014, fig.50), at the Regen Projects, Los Angeles (2014). In the latter video, participants confess their fears and ongoing loathing while wearing one of Wearing's signature masks. • Made an Honorary Fellow (2015) of the University of the Arts London.

Wearing's *Rock 'n' roll 70* (cat.88) self-portrait is exhibited for the first time at her solo exhibition at the Institut Valencià d'Art Modern in 2015. Also shown is the video installation, *Your views,* a project she began in 2013 and in which she invites people from across the world to submit a film recording the view from their window. An expanded version of the project, *A room with your views*, is included in the 2016 HOUSE/Brighton Festival. • In 2016 Wearing is given an Honorary Degree of Doctor of Birmingham City University.

Fig.48 Wearing trying on the mask that was made for *Self-portrait as my brother, Richard Wearing*, 2003

Fig.49 *A real Birmingham family* by Gillian Wearing, bronze sculpture, 2014

Fig.50 *Fear and loathing* by Gillian Wearing, 2014

Curator's acknowledgements

I am especially grateful to Gillian Wearing, who has been a great collaborator on this creative journey. Our research trip to Jersey, and subsequent conversations, gave me insight into Gillian's way of working and her sensitive response to Claude Cahun. I am also grateful to Jersey Heritage, holder of the Cahun archive, and in particular to Louise Downie and Val Nelson for generously sharing it, and their knowledge, with us. I should like to thank, too, all the lenders of these precious Cahun works, including: Jersey Heritage; Bibliothèque Marguerite Durand; Centre Pompidou – Musée national d'art moderne, Paris; a private lender courtesy of Jersey Heritage; Musée d'Art moderne de la Ville de Paris; Musée des Beaux-arts de Nantes; The Museum of Modern Art, New York; Victoria & Albert Museum, London; and Wilson Centre for Photography. In addition to these lenders, I would like to thank the Galerie nationale du Jeu de Paume, Paris – in particular, Muriel Rausch, Head of Publications – for their assistance.

Gillian Wearing has a loyal group of collectors internationally, and I am indebted to them and, of course, to Maureen Paley, who has been an enthusiastic supporter and lender to this exhibition. We would also like to extend our thanks to Shaun Caley Regen and Tanya Bonakdar, and the teams at Maureen Paley, London; Regen Projects, Los Angeles; and Tanya Bonakdar Gallery, New York, who have all contributed enormously in securing key works. The lenders include: Gillian Wearing; a private lender courtesy of Cecilia Dan Fine Art, Los Angeles; Government Art Collection, London; Heather Podesta Collection; Collection of Mario Testino; Nancy and Fred Poses courtesy Meredith Palmer Gallery Ltd, New York; Tanya Bonakdar Gallery, New York; Regen Projects, Los Angeles; Solomon R. Guggenheim Museum, New York; Tony Podesta Collection, Washington, DC and the Zabludowicz Collection, London.

Finally, I should like to thank the Director of the National Portrait Gallery, Nicholas Cullinan, for his support for the project from the outset, and others at the Gallery, in particular the exhibitions and design teams, including Eloise Stewart, Ulrike Wachsmann, Ian Gardner, Rosie Wilson and Sarah Tinsley for their significant contributions every step of the way. For their work on this catalogue, I should also like to thank Dawn Ades for her perceptive essay on Cahun and her work; Andrew Roff for his meticulous editing; Helen Armitage and Alison Effeny for copy-editing and proofreading respectively; Tanya Bentley, Mark Lynch and Ruth Müller-Wirth for their careful attention to detail; and designers Praline for their creative vision. A word of thanks, too, to Prudence Cuming Associates Ltd for new digital captures.

Sarah Howgate
Senior Curator of Contemporary Portraits,
National Portrait Gallery, London

Further reading

*exhibition catalogues

Claude Cahun

Downie, Louise (ed.), *Don't Kiss Me: The Art of Claude Cahun and Marcel Moore* (Tate, London, 2006; in association with Jersey Heritage Trust)

Doy, Gen, *Claude Cahun: A Sensual Politics of Photography* (I.B. Tauris, London and New York, 2007)

Kline, Katy, 'In or Out of the Picture: Claude Cahun and Cindy Sherman', *Mirror Images: Women, Surrealism and Self-representation*, ed. Whitney Chadwick (The MIT Press, Cambridge, Massachusetts, and London, 1998), pp.66–81

Leperlier, François, *Claude Cahun: L'écart et la métamorphose* (Jean-Michel Place Éditions, Paris, 1992)

— *Claude Cahun: L'Exotisme intérieur* (Fayard, Paris, 2006)

*Rice, Shelley (ed.), *Inverted Odysseys: Claude Cahun, Maya Deren, Cindy Sherman*, exh. cat. (The MIT Press, Cambridge, Massachusetts, and London, 1999)

Sprio, Margherita, 'Feminisms, Mirrors: Claude Cahun and Sarah Pucill – a Dialogue', *Moving Image Review & Art Journal* (*MIRAJ*), vol.4 (1–2), 2015, pp.260–7

**Mise en Scène: Claude Cahun, Tacita Dean, Virginia Nimarkoh*, exh. cat. (Institute of Contemporary Arts, London, 1994)

**Claude Cahun: Photographe*, exh. cat. (Musée d'Art moderne de la Ville de Paris, Paris, 1995)

**Claude Cahun*, exh. cat. (Institut Valencià d'Art Modern, Valencià, 2001)

**Claude Cahun*, exh. cat. (Jeu de Paume, Place de la Concorde, Paris, 2011)

Selected writings

Cahun, Claude, *Aveux non avenus* (Éditions du Carrefour, Paris, 1930). For an English translation: *Disavowals or Cancelled Confessions*, trans. Susan de Muth (Tate, London, 2007)

Cahun, Claude: *Écrits*, ed. François Leperlier (Jean-Michel Place Éditions, Paris, 2002)

Gillian Wearing

Ferguson, Russell et al., *Gillian Wearing* (Phaidon, London, 1999)

**Gillian Wearing: Sous Influence*, exh. cat. (Musée d'Art moderne de la Ville de Paris, Paris, 2001)

**Gillian Wearing*, exh. cat. (Fundación 'la Caixa', Madrid, 2001)

**Gillian Wearing: Mass Observation*, exh. cat. (Museum of Contemporary Art, Chicago, and Merrell, London, 2002)

**Living Proof,* exh. cat. (Australian Centre for Contemporary Art (ACCA), Melbourne, 2006)

Family History (Film and Video Umbrella and Maureen Paley, London, 2007; in association with Artists in the City, Reading, and Ikon Gallery, Birmingham)

**Gillian Wearing*, exh. cat. (Whitechapel Gallery and Ridinghouse, London, 2012)

**Gillian Wearing*, exh. cat. (Institut Valencià d'Art Modern, Valencià, 2015)

Exhibition list and picture credits

The National Portrait Gallery would like to thank the copyright holders for granting permission to reproduce works illustrated in this book. Every effort has been made to contact the holders of copyright material, and any omission will be corrected in future editions if the publisher is notified in writing.

Dimensions of Wearing's works are framed unless otherwise stated; dimensions of Cahun's are image size unless otherwise stated. All dimensions are given height × width × depth.

Plates

1 *Me: Me*
Gillian Wearing, 1991/2016; silver gelatin print, 513 × 433mm (unframed); Courtesy Maureen Paley, London, and Tanya Bonakdar Gallery, New York

2 *Self-portrait* from 'I am in training don't kiss me' series
Claude Cahun, c.1927; silver gelatin print, 104 × 76mm; Musée d'Art Moderne de la Ville de Paris; © Musée d'Art Moderne/Roger-Viollet

3 *Self-portrait* from 'I am in training don't kiss me' series
Claude Cahun, c.1927; silver gelatin print, 116 × 74mm

4 *Self-portrait* from 'I am in training don't kiss me' series
Claude Cahun, c.1927; copy print after an original silver gelatin print; Musée des Beaux-arts de Nantes; photo © RMN-Grand Palais/Gerard Blot

5 *Self-portrait* from 'I am in training don't kiss me' series
Claude Cahun, c.1927; silver gelatin print, 117 × 89mm

6 *Me as Cahun holding a mask of my face*
Gillian Wearing, 2012; silver gelatin print, 1556 × 1286 × 33mm; Courtesy Tanya Bonakdar Gallery, New York, Maureen Paley, London, and Regen Projects, Los Angeles

7 *At Claude Cahun's grave*
Gillian Wearing, 2015; silver gelatin print; Courtesy Maureen Paley, London

8 *Self-portrait (as a young girl)*
Claude Cahun, 1914; silver gelatin print, 176 × 235mm

9 *Self-portrait (reading, with* L'Image de la femme*)* (The image of woman*)*
Claude Cahun, 1915; silver gelatin print, 110 × 82mm

10 *Self-portrait (in an Orientalist setting)*
Claude Cahun, 1916; modern silver gelatin print from original negative, 120 × 90mm (negative); Private Collection

11 *Self-portrait (in turban)*
Claude Cahun, c.1913; silver gelatin print, 180 × 137mm (circular); Private Collection

12 *Self-portrait (hand on breast)*
Claude Cahun, c.1916; silver gelatin print, 180 × 101mm

13 *Self-portrait (seated on granite rocks)*
Claude Cahun, c.1915–17; sepia-toned silver gelatin print, 87 × 120mm

14 *Self-portrait (against granite wall)*
Claude Cahun, 1916; silver gelatin print, 118 × 89mm

15 *Self-portrait (shaved head, material draped across body)*
Claude Cahun, c.1920; modern silver gelatin print from original negative, 118 × 92mm (negative)

16 *Self-portrait (plaited fringe)*
Claude Cahun, 1917; sepia-toned silver gelatin print, 119 × 83mm

17 *Self-portrait (seated cross-legged on beach)*
Claude Cahun, 1923; silver gelatin print glued on to card, 161 × 213mm (image size); Musée d'Art Moderne de la Ville de Paris © Musée d'Art Moderne/Roger-Viollet

18 *Self-portrait (head between hands)*
Claude Cahun, 1920; silver gelatin print, 139 × 90mm

19 *Self-portrait (shaved head, looking over left shoulder)*
Claude Cahun, 1920; copy print after an original silver gelatin print

20 *Self-portrait (in profile, wearing corduroy jacket)*
Claude Cahun, c.1919; silver gelatin print, 238 × 179mm; Centre Pompidou – Musée National d'Art Moderne (no. inv.: AM 1993–146); Photo © Centre Pompidou, MNAM-CCI, Dist. RMN-Grand Palais/Philippe Migeat

21 *Self-portrait at seventeen years old*
Gillian Wearing, 2003; colour coupler print, 1156 × 920 x 32mm; Heather Podesta Collection

22 *Self-portrait*
Gillian Wearing, 1985; oil on board, 255 × 175mm; Courtesy the artist

23 *Me as an artist in 1984*
Gillian Wearing, 2014; colour coupler print, 1330 × 1610 × 32mm; Lent by the UK Government Art Fund. Purchased 2014

24 [pages 48–9] A selection of Polaroids from *My Polaroid years*
Gillian Wearing, 1988–2005; Polaroid photographs, 108 × 89mm each; Tony Podesta Collection, Washington DC

[pages 50–1] Installation shot from the exhibition *My Polaroid Years*, Tanya Bonakdar Gallery at ADAA, Park Avenue Armory, New York, March 2016 © Gillian Wearing, courtesy Maureen Paley, London, and Tanya Bonakdar Gallery, New York

25 *Aveux non avenus* cover
Claude Cahun in collaboration with Marcel Moore, published in Paris on 30 May 1930; book, 220 × 170 × 28mm (closed)

26 *Studies for a keepsake*
Claude Cahun, c.1925; four silver gelatin prints mounted on card, 140 × 450mm; Musée d'Art Moderne de la Ville de Paris © Musée d'Art Moderne/Roger-Viollet

27 *Aveux non avenus* photomontage prefacing chapter III *E.D.M. (Sex)*
Claude Cahun in collaboration with Marcel Moore, published in Paris on 30 May 1930; book, 220 × 170 × 28mm (closed)

28 *Aveux non avenus* frontispiece
Photomontage by Claude Cahun in collaboration with Marcel Moore. Photographed by Cahun in 1930, printed in 2004; platinum contact print made from 'half-plate'-sized glass, 180 × 130mm; Victoria and Albert Museum, London; given by Michael Hoppen;represented in catalogue by page from *Aveux non avenus* (see cat.25 for credit information)

29 *Aveux non avenus* photomontage prefacing chapter IX *I.O.U. (Self-pride)*
Photomontage by Claude Cahun in collaboration with Marcel Moore. Photographed by Cahun in 1930, printed in 2004; platinum contact print made from 'half-plate'-sized glass, 180 × 130mm; Victoria and Albert Museum, London; given by Michael Hoppen;represented in catalogue by page from *Aveux non avenus* (see cat.25 for credit information)

30 *Lucie au Kid (Lucie and Kid)*
Claude Cahun, c.1925; silver gelatin print, 120 × 90mm

31 *The artist's hand*
Gillian Wearing, 2012; traditional casting wax, 220 × 110 × 60mm; Courtesy the artist

32 *Untitled (four-hands image)*
Claude Cahun, c.1936; silver gelatin print, 251 × 196mm; Musée d'Art Moderne de la Ville de Paris; © Musée d'Art Moderne/Roger-Viollet

33 *My misfortune (left)*
Gillian Wearing, 2014; resin, marble dust, oil paint and indelible pen on wooden base with Perspex hood, 50 × 215 × 120mm (hand); Courtesy Maureen Paley, London, and Regen Projects, Los Angeles

34 *My fortune (right)*
Gillian Wearing, 2014; resin, marble dust, oil paint and indelible pen on wooden base with Perspex hood, 50 × 215 × 120mm (hand); Courtesy Maureen Paley, London, and Regen Projects, Los Angeles

35 *Entre nous (Between us) (feather, comb, matches and objects on sand)*
Claude Cahun, c.1930; silver gelatin print, 102 × 78mm

36 *Je tends les bras (I extend my arms)*
Claude Cahun, c.1932; modern silver gelatin print from original negative, 120 × 90mm (negative)

37 *Self-portrait (naked, reclining on sand with coiled seaweed)*
Claude Cahun, c.1930; silver gelatin print, 100 × 80mm

38 *Self-portrait (double exposure in a rock pool)*
Claude Cahun, c.1928; silver gelatin print, 181 × 130mm

39 *Self-portrait (with star-shaped pin)*
Claude Cahun, c.1930–9; silver gelatin print, 100 × 32mm; Wilson Centre for Photography; image: © Wilson Centre for Photography

40 *Self-portrait at twenty-seven years old*
Gillian Wearing, 2012; digital colour coupler print, 1956 × 368mm; Nancy and Fred Poses, New York, courtesy Meredith Palmer Gallery Ltd, New York

41 *Self-portrait as my mother, Jean Gregory*
Gillian Wearing, 2003; silver gelatin print, 1500 × 1310 × 32mm; collection Maureen Paley

42 *Self-portrait as my father, Brian Wearing*
Gillian Wearing, 2003; silver gelatin print, 1640 × 1305 × 32mm; Collection of Mario Testino

43 *Self-portrait as my grandmother, Nancy Gregory*
Gillian Wearing, 2006; silver gelatin print, 1610 × 1305 × 32mm; Courtesy the artist and Regen Projects, Los Angeles

44 *Self-portrait as my grandfather, George Gregory*
Gillian Wearing, 2006; silver gelatin print, 1610 × 1305 × 32mm; Courtesy the artist and Regen Projects, Los Angeles

45 *Self-portrait (as a dandy, head and shoulders)*
Claude Cahun, 1921–2; silver gelatin print, 237 × 150mm; The Museum of Modern Art, New York. Thomas Walther Collection. Gift of Mrs Leon Dabo, by exchange; digital image: The Museum of Modern Art, New York/Scala, Florence

46 *Self-portrait (seated cross-legged like Buddha)*
Claude Cahun, 1927; silver gelatin print, 120 × 90mm

47 *Self-portrait as my sister, Jane Wearing*
Gillian Wearing, 2006; colour coupler print, 1410 × 1160 × 32mm; Heather Podesta Collection

48 *Self-portrait as my brother, Richard Wearing*
Gillian Wearing, 2003; colour coupler print, 1910 × 1305 × 32mm; Heather Podesta Collection

49 *Self-portrait (in cupboard)*
Claude Cahun, c.1932; silver gelatin print, 112 × 85mm

50 *Self-portrait at three years old*
Gillian Wearing, 2004, edition 5/6 Chromogenic print, 1575 × 1299 × 32mm; Solomon R. Guggenheim Museum, New York Purchased with funds contributed by the International Director's Council and Executive Committee Members: Ruth Baum, Edythe Broad, Elaine Terner Cooper, Dimitris Daskalopoulos, Harry David, Gail May Engelberg, Shirley Fiterman, Nicki Harris, Dakis Joannou, Rachel Lehmann, Linda Macklowe, Peter Norton, Tonino Perna, Elizabeth

Richebourg Rea, Mortimer D.A. Sackler, Simonetta Seragnoli, David Teiger, Ginny Williams, and Elliot K. Wolk, and Sustaining Members: Tiqui Atencio, Linda Fischbach, Beatrice Habermann, Miryam Knutson, and Cargill and Donna MacMillan; with additional funds contributed by the Photography Committee 2004.125

51 *Me as Arbus*
Gillian Wearing, 2008; silver gelatin print, 1560 × 1330 × 32mm; Collection of Mario Testino

52 *Me as Warhol in drag with scar*
Gillian Wearing, 2010; silver gelatin print, 1560 × 1330 × 32mm; Heather Podesta Collection

53 *Self-portrait (full-length masked figure in cloak with masks)*
Claude Cahun, c.1928; modern silver gelatin print from original negative, 120 × 94mm (negative)

54 *Self-portrait of me now in mask*
Gillian Wearing, 2011; colour coupler print, 1240 × 980 × 30mm; Collection of Mario Testino

55 *Self-portrait (in headscarf with mask in background)*
Claude Cahun, c.1929; copy print after an original silver gelatin print; Musée des Beaux-arts de Nantes; Photo: © RMN-Grand Palais/Gerard Blot

56 *Self-portrait (kneeling, naked with mask)*
Claude Cahun, c.1928; silver gelatin print, 118 × 88mm

57 *Têtes de cristal (Crystal heads), British Museum, London*
Claude Cahun, June–July 1936; modern silver gelatin print from original negative, 118 × 92mm (negative)

58 *Me as mask*
Gillian Wearing, 2013; unique wax sculpture and wooden plinth, 560 × 140 × 100mm (sculpture without plinth); Private Collection, courtesy Cecilia Dan Fine Art

59 *Self-portrait*
Gillian Wearing, 2000; colour coupler print, 1720 × 1720 × 32mm; Zabludowicz Collection

60 *Self-portrait (in goggles)*
Claude Cahun, 1927; copy print after an original silver gelatin print; Musée des Beaux-arts de Nantes; Photo: © RMN-Grand Palais/Gerard Blot

61 *Dancing in Peckham*
Gillian Wearing, 1994; colour video with sound, 60 minutes (25 minute sequence repeated until end of tape); Lent by the UK Government Art Collection. Purchased 1997

62a *Self-portrait (on sea wall at La Rocquaise)*
Claude Cahun, 1947; silver gelatin print, 111 × 81mm

62b Contact sheets for *Self-portrait (on sea wall at La Rocquaise)*
Claude Cahun, 1947; silver gelatin print contact strip, 114 × 37mm (left) and 107 × 35mm (right)

63 *Self-portrait (as Monsieur in* Banlieu*)*
Claude Cahun, 1929; silver gelatin print, 111 × 89mm

64 *Self-portrait (as le Diable in* Le Mystère d'Adam*)*
Claude Cahun, 1929; silver gelatin print, 240 × 179mm; Musée d'Art moderne de la Ville de Paris © Musée d'Art Moderne/Roger-Viollet

65 *Self-portrait (as Elle in* Barbe-Bleue*)*
Claude Cahun, 1929; silver gelatin print, 235 × 181mm

66 *Self-portrait (aerial view on blanket)*
Claude Cahun, 1928; silver gelatin print, 105 × 82mm

67 *Self-portrait (aerial view on blanket)*
Claude Cahun, 1928; silver gelatin print, 106 × 81mm

68 *Self-portrait (reflected image in mirror with chequered jacket)*
Claude Cahun, 1927; silver gelatin print, 255 × 201mm; Wilson Centre for Photography; image: © Wilson Centre for Photography

69 *Mirror*
Gillian Wearing, 2016; Polaroid, 102 × 102mm; Courtesy Maureen Paley, London

70 *Self-portrait (in national dress)*
Claude Cahun, c.1938; silver gelatin print, 169 × 98mm; Musée d'Art Moderne de la Ville de Paris; © Musée d'Art Moderne/Roger-Viollet

71 *Self-portrait (naked with leaves)*
Claude Cahun, 1938; silver gelatin print, 111 × 84mm

72 *Self-portrait (with leopard skin)*
Claude Cahun, 1939; silver gelatin print, 110 × 80mm

73 *Self-portrait (lying on leopard skin)*
Claude Cahun, 1939; silver gelatin print, 84 × 110mm

74 *Self-portrait (in barn doorway)*
Claude Cahun, 1938; silver gelatin print, 112 × 85mm

75 *Self-portrait (in velvet dress, in front of La Rocquaise arch)*
Claude Cahun, 1939; silver gelatin print, 110 × 83mm

76 *Self-portrait (in cloak with cloaked figure)*
Claude Cahun, 1939; silver gelatin print, 110 × 85mm

77 *Self-portrait (with round frame)*
Claude Cahun, c.1938; silver gelatin print, 112 × 84mm

78 *Self-portrait (in window at La Rocquaise)*
Claude Cahun, c.1938; silver gelatin print, 110 × 90mm

79 *Self-portrait (standing and sitting in garden)*
Claude Cahun, 1939; silver gelatin print, 181 × 129mm

80 *Self-portrait (with Nazi badge between teeth)*
Claude Cahun, 1945; silver gelatin print, 133 × 83mm

81 *Self-portrait (with masked face and graveyard)*
Claude Cahun, c.1947; silver gelatin print, 85 × 60mm

82 *Le chemin des chats V (Cats' lane V)*
Claude Cahun, c.1948; silver gelatin print, 209 × 160mm

83 *Self-portrait (in doorway on La Rocquaise)*
Claude Cahun, 1937; silver gelatin print, 90 × 70mm

84 *Self-portrait (with cat, skull and gravestone)*
Claude Cahun, c.1947; silver gelatin print, 86 × 63mm

85 *Self-portrait (with skull and cigarette)*
Claude Cahun, 1947; silver gelatin print, 84 × 60mm

86 *Marcel Moore and Claude Cahun*
Claude Cahun, 1950; silver gelatin print, 135 × 85mm

87 *Me as a clock*
Gillian Wearing, 1990; metal, clock and photograph, 150mm (diameter) × 15mm; Courtesy the artist

88 *Rock 'n' roll 70*
Gillian Wearing, 2015; colour coupler print, 1310 × 1920 × 32mm; Courtesy Maureen Paley, London, Regen Projects, Los Angeles, Tanya Bonakdar Gallery, New York

89 *Me as my ideal self*
Gillian Wearing, 2012; acrylic on masonite in custom frame; ink on paper, photographs under glass; 1168 × 572 × 51mm (frame closed); 1168 × 1143 × 25mm (frame open); Courtesy the artist and Regen Projects, Los Angeles © Gillian Wearing, courtesy Maureen Paley, London, and Regen Projects, Los Angeles

90 *Me as a ghost*
Gillian Wearing, 2015; colour coupler print, 1315 × 915 × 32mm; Courtesy Maureen Paley, London, Regen Projects, Los Angeles, Tanya Bonakdar Gallery, New York

91 *Me as Mapplethorpe*
Gillian Wearing, 2009; silver gelatin print, 1590 × 1310 × 32mm; Collection of Mario Testino

92 *Rock 'n' roll 70 wallpaper*
Gillian Wearing, 2015; printed wallpaper; Courtesy Maureen Paley, London, Regen Projects, Los Angeles, Tanya Bonakdar Gallery, New York

93 *Nancy Gregory*
Gillian Wearing, 2002; framed monitor playing colour video with sound (2 minutes looped); Courtesy Maureen Paley, London, Regen Projects, Los Angeles, Tanya Bonakdar Gallery, New York

94 *My exquisite corpse*
Gillian Wearing, 2016; with Gary Hume (head), Michael Landy (torso), Gillian Wearing (legs); paper, acrylic, charcoal, ink, oil paint, colour coupler print, pencil, 2400 × 1520mm; Courtesy Maureen Paley, London; © Gary Hume © Michael Landy © Gillian Wearing, courtesy Maureen Paley, London, Regen Projects, Los Angeles, and Tanya Bonakdar Gallery, New York

Figures

1 *Marcel Moore (Suzanne Malherbe) and Claude Cahun (Lucy Schwob) reflected in mirror*
Claude Cahun, c.1920; silver gelatin print, 179 × 238mm

2 *Self-portrait reflected in mirror*
Gillian Wearing, 1984

3 *Shami Chakrabarti, Baroness Chakrabarti*
Gillian Wearing, 2011; silver gelatin print, 929 × 800mm; commission made possible by J.P. Morgan through the Fund for New Commissions, 2011 © National Portrait Gallery, London (NPG 6923)

4 *Me as Weegee*
Gillian Wearing, 2013; framed bromide print, 150 × 105mm (unframed); Maureen Paley, London, Regen Projects, Los Angeles, Tanya Bonakdar Gallery, New York

5 The gravestone of Cahun and Moore in St Brelade's Bay, Jersey.
Gillian Wearing, 2016

6 *Self-portrait (in sailor hat)*
Claude Cahun, c.1920; 89 × 60mm; Private Collection/Photo © Christie's Images/Bridgeman Images

7 *Maurice Schwob, Cahun's father*
Unknown photographer, 1917; Private Collection

8 *Tanja Ramm under a bell jar, France*
Lee Miller, 1930
© Lee Miller Archives, England 2016. All rights reserved

9 *Five-way portrait of Marcel Duchamp*
Marcel Duchamp, 1917; gelatin silver print, 87 × 140mm; Private Collection. Image courtesy Francis M. Naumann Fine Art, New York. © Succession Marcel Duchamp, 2016/DACS, London

10 *Que me veux-tu? (What do you want from me?)*
Claude Cahun, 1928; silver gelatin print, 180 × 230mm; Musée d'Art Moderne de la Ville de Paris; Musée d'Art Moderne/ Roger-Viollet

11 *Object*
Claude Cahun, 1936; wood, paint and hair, 137 × 107 × 160mm; Art Institute of Chicago, Illinois, USA/Through prior gift of Mrs. Gilbert W. Chapman/ Bridgeman Images

12 *Woman combing her hair*
Edgar Degas, c.1885; pastel on greyish-brown paper pasted on cardboard, 540 × 525mm; State Hermitage Museum, St Petersburg

13 *Marcel Duchamp as his alter-ego Rrose Sélavy*
Man Ray, 1921; © Man Ray Trust/ADAGP – DACS/Telimage – 2016

14 Masks used in *Me as Cahun holding a mask of my face* (left, cat.6) and *Self-portrait at twenty-seven years old* (right, cat.40) by Gillian Wearing, 2011 and 2012; silicone, hair, oil paint, 170 × 145 × 90mm each; Courtesy the artist

15 *Self-portrait (masked, slumped in chair)*
Claude Cahun, c.1928; silver gelatin print, 100 × 76mm; purchase and anonymous promised gift. Acc.no.: 763.1998. © 2016. Digital image, The Museum of Modern Art, New York/ Scala, Florence

16 Portrait bronze of Cahun
Chana Orloff, 1921; Bronze, 406mm; © Estate of Chana Orloff, 2016/DACS, London 2016. Photo © Jersey Heritage

17 *Marcel Moore (reflected in mirror)*
Claude Cahun, 1928; negative, 107 × 82mm (negative size)

18 Self-portrait *(double head image as Elle in* Barbe-Bleue*)*
Claude Cahun, 1929; silver gelatin print, 138 × 86mm

19 *Self-portrait (with globe)*
Claude Cahun, c.1927; silver gelatin print, 117 × 88mm; Detroit Institute of Arts, Founders Society Purchase, Albert and Peggy de Salle Charitable Trust and DeRoy Photographic Acquisition Endowment Fund; Detroit Institute of Arts, USA/Bridgeman Images

20 Wearing in St Brelade's Bay, Jersey
Sarah Howgate, 2016

21 Wearing posing as her mother without a mask during the staging of *Self-portrait as my mother, Jean Gregory*, 2003;
Gillian Wearing, 2003; Gillian Wearing

22 Andy Warhol filming *Chelsea Girls* in New York
Santi Visalli, 4 May 1966; Santi Visalli/ Archive Photos/Getty Images

23 *Family History* catalogue cover
Gillian Wearing, 2007; published by Maureen Paley, London, and Film and Video Umbrella; Maureen Paley, London

24 Wearing in hairdressing magazine *Hair and Beauty*, June 1987
Kriss Hass

25 Fashion illustration
Marcel Moore, 1915; © Jersey Heritage

26 Wearing looking at La Rocquaise
Sarah Howgate, 2016

27 *Self-portrait*
Claude Cahun; published in the journal *Bifur*, no.5, April 1930; Private Collection

28 *Shop window van den Bergh* (Launch of *Aveux non avenus*)
Unknown photographer, June 1930;
© Jersey Heritage

29 *Frontières humaines* cover (1929) with the drawing *What do you want from me?*
Georges Ribemont-Dessaignes (editor), 1929; book; Private Collection

30 *Documents Surréalistes*
Maurice Nadeau, 1948; Private Collection

31 Still from *Un chien andalou*
Luis Buñuel and Salvador Dalí, 1929; Private Collection

32 Surrealists in London
Unknown photographer, 1936
© Jersey Heritage

33 *Self-portrait (as a dandy, three-quarter length)*
Claude Cahun, 1921–2; Private Collection

34 *Posturing: Drag*, Martha Wilson, 1972/96
Photograph by Doug Waterman; colour photograph and text, 280 × 203mm;
P•P•O•W Gallery, New York
Courtesy the artist and P•P•O•W, New York

35 Suzanne Malherbe
Claude Cahun, 1915

36 'Les Jeux uraniens' manuscript
Claude Cahun, 1914

37 *Héroïnes* manuscript with *Cinderella slipper*, decorated using typewriter keys
Claude Cahun, 1925

38 Claude Cahun in her Paris apartment, 7 bis rue Notre-Dame-des-Champs
Unknown photographer, 1923
© Jersey Heritage

39 Claude Cahun in the doorway at La Rocquaise
Unknown photographer, after 1938; negative, 80 × 110mm (negative size)
© Jersey Heritage

40 Propaganda leaflets made during the German Occupation of Jersey
Claude Cahun and Marcel Moore, 1940–4

41 Claude Cahun (left) with an unidentified woman outside the mini-exhibition held at José Corti bookshop, Paris, for the launch of *Aveux non avenus*
Unknown photographer, June 1930;
Jersey Heritage Collection;
© Jersey Heritage

42 Interior at La Rocquaise
Unknown photographer, after 1937;
Jersey Heritage Collection;
© Jersey Heritage

43 Gillian and her friend Michele Markham in Birmingham
Kimberly Harrington, 1981

44 Wearing in Earl's Court, London
Unknown photographer, 1984

45 *Signs that say what you want them to say and not signs that say what someone else wants you to say*
Gillian Wearing, 1992–3; C-type print mounted on aluminium, 1330 × 930mm;
Maureen Paley, London

46 *Observer Magazine*, September 2000
© Guardian News & Media Ltd 2016;
cover photograph © Gautier Deblonde

47 Michael Landy and Gillian Wearing in photo booth with Raphael effect, 2001
Gillian Wearing

48 Wearing trying on the mask that was made for *Self-portrait as my brother, Richard Wearing*
Gillian Wearing, 2003; Courtesy the artist

49 *A real Birmingham family*
Gillian Wearing, 2014; bronze, 1920 × 2525 × 910mm (with plinth), 1650 × 2250 × 700mm (without plinth);
Photo: Courtesy Birmingham City Council, Arts Council England and Ikon

50 *Fear and loathing*
Gillian Wearing, 2014; two-screen colour video with sound (44 minutes 45 seconds)

Index

Note page numbers in bold refer to information contained in captions.